RAY HERNÁNDEZ-DURÁN, RICHARD SANTOS, MICHAEL TRUJILLO, IRENE VASQUEZ, and MATTHEW GOODWIN, **Series Editors**

In keeping with the transdisciplinary mission of the Southwest Hispanic Research Institute (SHRI) at the University of New Mexico, the Contextos Series publishes books that deepen our understanding of the historical, social, political, and cultural issues that impact Latinas and Latinos. Topics may span regional, national, and transnational contexts. We invite scholarship in Chicana and Chicano Studies, the social sciences, public policy, the humanities, health and natural science, and other professional fields.

Also available in the Contextos Series:

Joaquín Ortega: Forging Pan-Americanism at the University of New Mexico by Russ Davidson

Making Aztlán: Ideology and Culture of the Chicana and Chicano Movement, 1966-1977 by Juan Gómez-Quiñones and Irene Vásquez

Laura Elena Belmonte

University of New Mexico Press
Albuquerque

BORDERLAND BRUTALITIES

Violence and Resistance along the US-Mexico Borderlands in Literature, Film, and Culture

© 2024 by the University of New Mexico Press

All rights reserved. Published 2024.
Printed in the United States of America

ISBN 978-0-8263-6612-2 (cloth)
ISBN 978-0-8263-6613-9 (pdf)

Library of Congress Cataloging in Publication data is on file with the Library of Congress.

Founded in 1889, the University of New Mexico sits on the traditional homelands of the Pueblo of Sandia. The original peoples of New Mexico—Pueblo, Navajo, and Apache—since time immemorial have deep connections to the land and have made significant contributions to the broader community statewide. We honor the land itself and those who remain stewards of this land throughout the generations and also acknowledge our committed relationship to Indigenous peoples. We gratefully recognize our history.

Cover illustration and frontispiece: Salvador Barajas, *Love Has No Borders*, 2017. Courtesy of the artist and Enrique Morones and the Border Angels organization.

Designed by Isaac Morris

Composed in Malaga and Noka

I dedicate this book to my sons,
Alejandro and Mateo,
and my wonderful husband,
Alfonso.
I love you.

CONTENTS

ACKNOWLEDGMENTS / xi

INTRODUCTION / 1

CHAPTER ONE. The Life of Teresa Urrea and the Yaqui Resistance Represented in Luis Alberto Urrea's Novel *The Hummingbird's Daughter* (2005) / 14

CHAPTER TWO. Capitalism and Complicity between the US Government and Railroad Corporations along the US-Mexico Borderlands / 35

CHAPTER THREE. "May We Break the Spell of the Official Story": The Criminalization of Refugees of Color Represented in Demetria Martínez's *Mother Tongue* (1994) and *Confessions of a Berlitz-Tape Chicana* (2005) / 56

CHAPTER FOUR. Priestess y *Pastora*: Transnational Female Spiritual Leadership in Ana Castillo's *So Far from God* (1993) and María Amparo Escandón's *Esperanza's Box of Saints* (1998) / 80

CHAPTER FIVE. The Coatlicue State and Moebius Strip: Mirrors and Mirroring in Artwork of the US-Mexico Border / 106

CHAPTER SIX. Making Waves in "Tranquil Waters": Chicanafuturism and the Invisibilization of Violence / 127

EPILOGUE. Fibroblast Migration and Borderlands Consciousness / 149

NOTES / 153

BIBLIOGRAPHY / 169

INDEX / 177

ACKNOWLEDGMENTS

Yo no creo en fronteras, yo cruzaré, yo cruzaré, yo cruzaré!
— "La Bamba Rebelde" by Las Cafeteras

I have to confess that I have looked forward to writing an acknowledgments section because I am truly so grateful for the village of people that have supported me as I wrote this book. I first wrote a proposal conceptualizing the main ideas of this book in January 2020, with the goal of finishing a manuscript by the end of the year. Little did I know that that year our whole world would change, and my book writing plans along with it. Despite the COVID-19 global pandemic, I had a group of cheerleaders who were invested in seeing this book come to be a reality.

My husband and family are the first I must thank. Alfonso, my husband and best friend, was my sounding board where I could talk through ideas, as well as my parenting partner as we navigated a pandemic with two children under the age of five. He supported me, heard me out, read my chapters, and encouraged me when I was unsure whether I would finish this book, all while he was navigating being a physician and first responder during the COVID-19 pandemic. I quite literally could not have done this book project without Alfonso: you are amazing, and I love you so much. Also, I want to thank my parents, Elena and Luis Maldonado, and my suegros, Armida and Hector Belmonte, who are truly an inspiration for this book because they are immigrants that have worked hard their entire lives, and also as grandparents to my children that supported me in help with childcare. Muchísimas gracias por todo, los quiero. I want to also thank and honor my Lely, Virginia Molina, who migrated in the seventies to this country from Mexico alone with two young daughters, one of whom would become my mother. Te quiero mucho, mi Lely hermosa, mueves montañas con tu valentía y amor.

My village also comprised friends and colleagues who read my chapters, gave me feedback, and also cheered me on as I struggled to finish this book. At the risk of forgetting someone, I want to thank Myrriah Gómez, Vanessa Fonseca-Chávez, Jesus Rosales, Natalia Toscano, Karen Roybal, Arifa Raza, Elizabeth González Cárdenas, Jose Luis Serrano Nájera, and Doris Careaga-Coleman. I also specifically want to thank my department chair, Irene Vasquez, for her constant support.

It is crucial to also thank UNM Press acquisition editor Elise McHugh for being so kind, approachable, and helpful in this process. Working with Elise has been a true joy.

I also want to thank the University of New Mexico's Office of the Vice President for Research for the book subvention funding I received through their WeR1 Faculty Success Program. This program funds faculty whose projects, research, and scholarship were affected by the COVID-19 pandemic so they may recover. I also wish to thank the University of New Mexico's Research Allocations Committee for granting me a book subvention. With these book subventions, I was able to hire a wonderful copyeditor, Alix Genter, who did an amazing job. I am truly grateful to Alix for her incredible work. Additionally, I wish to thank the University of New Mexico Center for Regional Studies, which supported me with this book's indexing costs.

Finally, I want to thank the artists that have so graciously given permission for their artwork to be reproduced in this book. Their work is truly inspiring, allowing us to get glimpses into a world in which the border wall doesn't separate, doesn't cause pain, and doesn't oppress. Thank you to Salvador Barajas, the artist who painted the mural *Love Has No Borders*, installed in Chicano Park, San Diego, California, and commissioned by Dr. Enrique Morones and the Border Angels organization. Also, thank you to Ana Teresa Fernandez, Margarita Certeza Garcia, Marcos Ramirez ERRE, and Dr. Ronald Rael. Your creativity and imagination are gifts to our communities.

INTRODUCTION

In the late morning on August 3, 2019, I was scrolling through social media and giving my two-year-old son lunch when breaking news about an active shooter at a Walmart in El Paso, Texas, started rolling in. As more information was released throughout the day, I learned that this man wrote a hate-filled screed posted on an online message board called 8chan. In this horrifying rant, he glorified then President Donald Trump and the shooter of Christchurch Mosque in New Zealand, went on a racist diatribe decrying a "Hispanic invasion," endorsed violence against Latinos, and promoted the great replacement theory—a white supremacist theory that claims white populations are being culturally and demographically replaced by non-Europeans. The screed's author killed twenty-three people and injured twenty-three more in that Walmart. Some of them were Mexican nationals that lived in Ciudad Juárez and were doing their back-to-school shopping in El Paso.

While there are many, many terrible incidents of gun violence in the United States, this particular incident scared me to my core. This shooter traveled to the US-Mexico border town of El Paso from Dallas, Texas—a nine-hour drive—to go on a killing spree targeting Mexicans: he was out to kill people like me and my family. Being a person of color means being racialized in this way: the interpretation of our very existence is done through biases and assumptions, which can embolden bigots to enact violence against our communities. My husband and my older son are dark-skinned, and so while my light skin affords me great privilege, I am deeply aware that my dark-skinned family contends with racism often. My thoughts in the wake of the El Paso mass shooting were: What if it happens where I live? What if a copycat of the El Paso shooter has their own rampage in our town, in a store where I am shopping with my husband and son? Given the rise of openly white supremacist groups, our fears could potentially become a reality. They already did in El Paso on August 3, 2019.

How does structural violence, such as the genocide of Indigenous people by European settlers or governments militarizing efforts to keep the border inaccessible, relate to the El Paso shooting? Some would argue that these are separate, that the shooter was a mentally disturbed "lone wolf"—a euphemism used time and again to justify the shooting sprees of white men as individualized incidents and not part of a structural problem. However, drawing on a long history of politically scapegoating Hispanic/Latinx communities as well as other racialized groups for society's ills, the shooter's manifesto parrots the racist anti-immigrant rhetoric put forth by those who espouse white supremacy.[1] Blaming immigrant communities for the nation's woes and accusing them of using resources and taking jobs has always been part and parcel of the structural violence inflicted upon them. This, too, is built into how they are racialized.

Living in communities of color in the US-Mexico borderlands is living with this reality of racialization and, as a result, violence. By "US-Mexico borderlands," I am referring to regions north and south of the border, what some call "border states," such as Texas, New Mexico, Arizona, and California in the United States and Baja California, Sonora, Chihuahua, Coahuila, Nuevo León, and Tamaulipas in Mexico. While the border is a line dividing the region, the communities on both sides are deeply connected. Gloria Anzaldúa called the US-Mexico border a "1,950 mile-long open wound," writing: "But the skin of the earth is seamless / The sea cannot be fenced / *el mar* does not stop at borders."[2] This book is an extension of Anzaldúa's poetic declaration. The US-Mexico border is a gash on the skin of the earth, a place where violence is enacted daily by state agencies and capitalistic hegemonies to exploit the land and profit from the border-wound. It is violence that is hurled upon border communities from outside the community: it is not inherent to border communities.

This violence is also structural. From European settlers'

sixteenth-century genocide of the Indigenous tribes they encountered in the region to the twenty-first-century Mexican and US nation-states' militarizing efforts to prevent asylum seekers from impoverished and war-stricken countries from reaching the United States, hegemonies have used their power to authorize violence against the borderlands' most marginalized groups. This external and structural violence seeps into the communities they brutalize and exploit, creating an ideology of the oppressor that promises access to what José David Saldívar calls the "imagined community of a nation."[3] In this imagined community, there are those who belong in the nation and those who don't. It has been clear from most of the history of the US-Mexico borderlands that those who "belong" and have rights are white, male, and wealthy. This idea of an imagined community of a nation is a dangerous tool used to legitimize violence against those existing outside the designated parameters of belonging—precisely those communities that have already been ostracized from the national imagined community.

And while the violence existing in the US-Mexico borderlands is wrought by hegemonies such as US and Mexican governments and powerful private corporations, it is the communities that inhabit them that have been depicted as inherently violent. From menacing images of people crossing the border portrayed as criminals to stories of cartel violence, these conceptualizations fill the imaginations of those outside these racialized border communities and strengthen damaging perceptions of local borderlands people and places. In this book I argue that the violence experienced in the borderlands is not inherent to its communities but rather to hegemonies like the US and Mexican governments, for-profit corporations, and the policies and systems that these powerful entities put in place. Angie Chabram-Dernersesian lays this out quite plainly: "Indeed, [the social and ethnic 'other' has] been targeted and reconfigured, and obligated to mark the outer limits of US citizenship—a formulation of 'Americanness' which takes aim at the traditionally undocumented, the newly documented, and those with documents/ papeles. This formulation constructs these groups as archetypal 'illegal aliens' who are not deserving of full participation within American society, notwithstanding their contributions, their documents and their historic claims to the territory."[4] This reconfiguration of making racialized borderlands people foreign and "other" enables powerful entities such as governments and corporations in their violent efforts to marginalize and criminalize them.

In defiance of such marginalization, Saldívar develops the term "disruptive cultural mappings," moving the US-Mexico borderlands from the periphery to the center of this discussion of state violence, nationhood, racism, capitalism, and misogyny. Repositioning the narrative of the imagined community of a nation from Washington, DC, and Mexico City to the periphery, Saldívar unsettles a national identity and origin story, positing, "How is the imagined community of a nation . . . disrupted and customized by materially hybrid US-Mexico borderland subjectivities?"[5] The imagined community of a nation both designs and legitimizes parameters of belonging: how is the imagined community of a nation further disrupted when borderlands subjectivities are the foundation of a borderlands consciousness? In this book, I intend to build on this question and Saldívar's concept of a "borderlands consciousness," a consciousness that denounces the violence inherent in the creation of the imagined community of a nation and calls the borderlands community to action through resistance of this violence to lead a dignified and decolonial existence. Borderlands consciousness is central to the argument and heart of this book: the cultural production that I explore and analyze in this book was, and is, produced by borderlands artists, writers, activists, and community members who love the US-Mexico borderlands, have pride and knowledge of their history in this geographic space, recognize the resilience and power of racialized communities, and actively denounce the violence brought about on their communities by powerful hegemonies. They also have a knowledge of power structures that are exclusive of communities of color on the US-Mexico borderlands, what Saldívar calls the "imagined community of a nation."

The exclusive nature of who belongs in this imagined

community of a nation leads to a power structure that perpetuates violence even as it, in Chela Sandoval's words, "democratizes oppression." This means that oppression can be carried out by anyone in a society; any "citizen-subject" can perpetuate violence on behalf of the hegemony. Sandoval argues that a "global structure" has replaced what Foucault called a "sovereign structure." Instead of having a sovereign structure, an earlier hierarchical system of power organized with kings and queens at the top and a peasant class at the bottom, Sandoval positions the global postmodern structure on a horizontal plane in the form of a flattened grid. She explains, "Because [the citizen-subjects] are horizontally located, it appears as if such politicized identities-as-positions can equally access their own racial-, sexual-, national-, or gender-unique forms of social power. Such constituencies are then perceived as speaking 'democratically' to and against each other in a lateral, horizonal—not pyramidal—exchange, although from spatially differing geographic, class, age, sex, race, or gender locations."[6] According to this formulation, the democratization of oppression among persons with various marginalized subjectivities allows them certain "quotients of power"; simply put, some have certain amounts of power over others by virtue of their status, race, gender, sexuality, and so forth, and therefore form a part of the imagined community of a nation (or at least aspire proximity to it). Others with subjectivities that do not align with the dominant culture, which is white, heteropatriarchal, and enjoys citizen status, are then pushed to the outskirts of this flattened grid.[7]

In the US-Mexico borderlands, there exists a higher quotient of power for those who are male, white, heterosexual, and Christian, and those who ascribe to ideologies that center these subjectivities—that is, even persons of color who aspire to proximity to power and whiteness. In contrast, Brown, Black, queer, undocumented, immigrant, and impoverished communities' quotients of power are minimal or nonexistent. Consequently, these groups are marginalized on the grid of the global postmodern power structure and subject to perpetual violence under hegemonic authority. An example of quotients of power multiplying is when hegemonies like the US government create enforcement agencies such as Customs and Border Patrol (CBP) and Immigration and Customs Enforcement (ICE) filled with persons whose "identities-as-positions" have higher quotients of social power; that is, they have United States citizenship.

Violence is impelling entire groups of people to actively center themselves to gain power over others and push those who are not like them to the margins. Put differently, marginalization constitutes structural violence, a term further developed by noted peace studies scholar Johan Galtung in his work on defining different types of violence and how these are the antithesis of peace. I draw on Galtung's definition of structural violence to develop this argument throughout the book. Galtung wrote extensively about how violence manifests in various ways, not just the somatic, or physical, ways that come to mind when we think of the term *violence*. In his definition, violence is *"the cause of the difference between the potential and the actual*, between what could have been and what is. Violence is that which increases the distance between the potential and the actual, and that which impedes the decrease of this distance . . . when the potential is higher than the actual is by definition *avoidable* and when it is avoidable, then violence is present."[8] In other words, violence is preventing an entity, be it a human being, a space or place, or wildlife, from being at its very best. It is the destruction of human potential: the potential to thrive, to grow, and to live fully. A metaphor that aptly describes this definition of violence regards a flower which grows well and healthily in its flowerpot: putting the flower in the dark, deliberately not watering it, letting it stay outside in a winter storm, and allowing rot in the soil to eat at its roots are all acts of violence. Galtung also offers examples to explain his definition of violence: when literacy in a population is lower than it could be, that population does not reach its potential, which facilitates the presence of violence.

There are differences between physical violence, what Galtung calls "somatic violence," the "deprivation of health . . . with killing as the extreme form," and nonphysical violence, or "structural violence."[9] Galtung defines structural violence as "the violence [that] is built into the structure and shows up as unequal power and consequently as unequal life chances."[10] Structural violence rationalizes policies and attitudes that are harmful toward a particular group as "the way things are"—or, more precisely, "the way *those people* are." It thus produces derogatory conceptualizations of marginalized communities, those who are not part of the imagined community of the nation, to justify the violence they face.

Galtung furthers his explanation of structural violence by juxtaposing it with what he calls "personal violence." He writes, "We shall refer to the type of violence where there is an actor that commits the violence as *personal* or *direct*, and to violence where there is no such actor as *structural* or *indirect*."[11] If the definition of violence is when a human being is prevented from reaching their potential, something that could have been avoided, then structural violence is present when whole groups of people are prevented from reaching their potential when it is avoidable. Misunderstanding the difference between structural and somatic violence may be the reason why so many misunderstand the concept of racism in the United States. Racism is not just personal attacks; it is structural violence enacted against entire groups of people that are racialized in ways that curtail their life expectancy, financial survival, and ability to provide safety for their children.

Structural violence is ever present against immigrants, as they are racialized as Brown and Black people that "don't follow the rules" and take resources from "those who deserve them," again drawing on understandings of entitlement and worth within the imagined community of a nation. Nicole Guidotti-Hernández writes at length about this in her book *Unspeakable Violence: Remapping U.S. and Mexican National Imaginaries* when discussing the story of Juanita/Josefa in a tourist magazine that in passing mentions the violent lynching of a Mexican woman in 1885. Guidotti-Hernández denounces what she calls a "banality of evil" of how normalized violence toward communities of color has become, even to the point of passively mentioning a violent act in, of all places, a tourism magazine.[12] And so we can see that these acts of normalizing of violence, both somatic and structural, are very old, as old as the US-Mexico borderlands themselves, and have the illogical effect of representing the communities of color that inhabit them as persistently foreign, even though many have deep ancestral roots in the region. Moreover, this marginalization of borderlands communities has led to enduring poverty as a result of structural racism and corruption. This is true on both sides of the border, as the US and Mexican governments have each enacted violence toward borderlands communities.

Racializing borderlands communities—othering them with the notion that they are foreign—brings forth a slew of violent legislation and policies that target them specifically. This violence manifests in many ways, such as in navigating the immigration system as an asylum seeker. There is also the violence that goes unprosecuted and unpunished, as with the femicides in Ciudad Juárez at the turn of the twentieth century. And finally, borderlands communities face capitalist violence when governments collude with private corporations to exploit cheap labor, utilize lax or nonexistent environmental laws, and prosecute those who protest capitalistic projects that endanger communities of color. The violence directed toward US-Mexico borderlands communities, wildlife, and landscapes ranges from literal acts of terror like the El Paso shooting to decades of impunity and corruption.

This book examines structural violence through its representations in the cultural production of US-Mexico borderlands communities. In doing so, it responds to Saldívar's call to center the borderlands in cultural theory, to "redraw the borders between folklore and the counterdiscourses of marginality, between 'everyday' culture and 'high' culture, and between 'people with culture' and 'people between culture.'"[13] By highlighting the cultural production of people from borderlands communities—particularly representations of how they experience hegemonic violence—I aim to advance Saldívar's project of remapping what constitutes "culture."

Saldívar discusses a "construction of borderland subjectivities" in which cultural production by borderlands communities represents in literature the experiences of these communities.[14] However, adding to this important work of studying borderlands subjectivities is distinguishing between culture and its production through these marginalized communities' understandings of their oppression, its sources, and how to resist it. Saldívar explains this distinction by employing Richard Johnson's differentiation between subjectivity and consciousness, wherein subjectivity "focuses on the 'who I am' or, as important, the 'who we are' of culture," while "the notion of a consciousness of self [is] an active mental and moral self-production."[15] This distinction is important in the study of US-Mexico borderlands communities, as the borderlands subjectivity is utilized to develop awareness within the community, a borderland consciousness. If culture is lived experience, as Chicano anthropologist Renato Rosaldo argues, then cultural production involves awareness of and engagement with the experiences one has lived in a way that produces art, literature, film, music, and other creative work.[16]

Elke Zobl and Elisabeth Klaus's discussion of cultural production offers further clarity about this distinction:

> Producing culture actively, thus, entails to think about the stance, the point of departure from which we act. It requires to think of the values, collective norms and invisible rules that guide our behaviour and to reflect on the social and cultural positioning of our activities. Finally, it encompasses a claim to participate in the formulation of the norms and values that govern society, to take part in its decision-making process about who or what counts as important or unimportant, as good or bad and to change the rules by which social and cultural relations are reinforced.[17]

Cultural production is a deliberate and purposeful act that, in this book, is very much meant to convey a message of borderlands consciousness. Artists and writers from the US-Mexico borderlands produce culture about their lived experience—that is, their borderlands subjectivity—which allows them, as Zobl and Klaus say, to reflect on the culture, participate in its formulation, and decide which values are important to include. Cultural production thus serves as a mirror as well as a sounding board for a borderland consciousness.

The study of US-Mexico borderlands cultural production illuminates themes of nation-building, citizenship (who gets to be part of the national imagined community and who does not), the justification of somatic violence at the site of the US-Mexico border, and the invisibilization of entire communities in order to exploit them. The project of nation-building includes an official narrative and definition of citizenship that details a model citizen—that is, a citizen that encapsulates the hegemonic values of national identity. The United States' origin mythology lies in the story of the founding fathers and their fight for independence, arguing that "all men are created equal," when it is clear this merely refers to white, wealthy slaveholders and landowners. In Mexico, the origin mythology of European conquest and the birth of the mestizo and the legal codification of patriarchal family values have been used to justify violence against groups of people that do not fit within the parameters of the ideal Mexican citizen, particularly cisgender and transgender women, queer people, and Indigenous communities. Through analyses of various cultural productions from the US-Mexico borderlands, this book explores these forms of violence, from the creation and protection of the imagined community of a nation and nation-building efforts that put its mythology into effect, to nation-states' complicity with private corporations to increase this so-called imagined community's wealth.

Chapter 1 examines Chicano writer Luis Alberto Urrea's historical novel *The Hummingbird's Daughter* (2005). The novel features Teresa (Teresita) Urrea, a well-known healer in the US-Mexico borderlands at the turn of the twentieth century, and the author's great aunt. As a *curandera* (a faith healer with hybrid spiritual beliefs rooted in Catholicism and Indigenous spiritualities), Teresa helped influence political rebellion among Indigenous groups fighting against Mexican government officials in the early twentieth century.

Her actions lead to her political persecution and ultimately her exile to the United States. I argue in this chapter that *The Hummingbird's Daughter* is a cultural production that represents both somatic violence (e.g., arrest, exile) and structural violence (e.g., the use of spies, military interventions at sites of faith healing) sanctioned by the Mexican state.

Chapter 2 analyzes issues surrounding the construction of the Southern Pacific railway in the late nineteenth and early twentieth centuries through María Amparo Ruiz de Burton's novel *The Squatter and the Don* (1885) and Daniel Venegas's novel *Las aventuras de Don Chipote; o, Cuando los pericos mamen* (1928). These cultural productions represent somatic violence (e.g., exploitation of laborers) as well as structural violence (e.g., legislation funding railroad construction and giving railroad companies public land that formerly belonged to marginalized communities; legalizing discriminatory medical procedures; legalizing slavery through vagrancy and anti-Indigenous laws) sanctioned by the United Sates government to further its efforts of nation-building and settler colonialism.

Chapter 3 focuses on Demetria Martínez's novel *Mother Tongue* (1994) and memoir *Confessions of a Berlitz-Tape Chicana* (2005) to analyze US asylum and sanctuary laws and Martínez's work in the sanctuary movement of the 1980s. The novel and memoir are cultural productions that depict somatic violence (e.g., the persecution and deportation of Central American asylum seekers) and structural violence (e.g., the use of the legal code to differentiate between *refugee* and *asylum seeker* to deny asylum to Brown and Black asylum seekers) sanctioned by the US government. I argue that the United States utilizes a language of criminalization to justify denying refugees entry into the country as well as persecute those who attempt to enter or are already there. This leads to the criminalization and racialization of refugees of color.

Chapter 4 examines how the mother figure in Ana Castillo's novel *So Far from God* (1993) and María Amparo Escandón's novel *Esperanza's Box of Saints* (1999) crosses national boundaries and challenges the notion of borders itself. Breaking with oppressive traditions, here the mother is a transnational subject who defies notions of citizenship. These representations portray the mother as the spiritual leader and protector of the home and community. She serves as an intermediary between that which is secular and that which is sacred, and transgresses borders through her role as a priestess and pastor. Among the borders she resists are the parameters of acceptable citizenship and the imagined community of a nation.

Chapter 5 explores the Coatlicue state and Moebius strip as useful theoretical frameworks for analyzing mirror and mirroring art installed on the US-Mexico border wall. This inquiry will consider the effects of mirroring and reflection presented in Ana Teresa Fernández's social sculpture *Borrando la Frontera* (Erasing the Border) (2011), the performance piece *Re/flecting the Border* (2017) by Margarita Certeza Garcia and Marcos Ramírez ERRE, and Ronald Rael's installation *Teeter-Totter Wall* (2019). These pieces all demonstrate resistance to the violence that the US-Mexico border wall brings to the region's communities, wildlife, and landscape. They are a clear and impactful denunciation of the border wall itself as violent. Here, the structural violence lies within laws and policies that enable the US government to build a wall that is clearly a militaristic tool to keep communities separate and that creates environmental hazards, as well as those they choose to ignore to equal effect.

Chapter 6 engages Chicanafuturism, which offers a critique of the past and present treatment of Brown and Black persons laboring along the US-Mexico borderlands. The chapter reflects upon the invisibilized transborder labor represented in three Chicanafuturist narratives, as technological advancements in fictional futures allow labor to be extracted from Brown bodies that are not seen. In Alex Rivera's *Sleep Dealer* (2008), workers in Mexico are hooked up to machines that control worker robots in the United States; in Rosaura Sánchez and Beatrice Pita's novel *Lunar Braceros, 2125–2148* (2009), a racialized workforce is sent to the moon to dispose of Earth's nuclear waste; and finally, in Alejandro Morales's *The Rag Doll Plagues* (1991), inhabitants of Mexico City are exploited and literally bled to heal the diseases of those residing in the nation of Lamex, a futuristic combination of the American Southwest and western Mexico. These narratives centering the exploitation of racialized, invisible labor expose and condemn the very real invisibilized transborder labor along the US-Mexico borderlands.

Cultural productions are an epistemological treasure trove that tell the stories of the communities they come from, share the value systems they embrace, and resist the powers that enact violence against them. Literature, music, film, and art are manifestations of human experiences—in this case, the experiences of communities of the US-Mexico borderlands. How they have used cultural production to denounce the violences they have faced— structural, capitalistic, environmental, somatic—is at the center of this book. My intention is to weave together an artistic genealogy of this resistance that pays homage to the dignity and everyday lives of *la gente fronteriza*.[18] Dignity in the face of structural and somatic violence is to be celebrated, but not required for la gente fronteriza to live in peace, to exist as they are, and to enjoy their cultural landscape, their *querencia*.

CHAPTER ONE

THE LIFE OF TERESA URREA AND THE YAQUI RESISTANCE REPRESENTED IN LUIS ALBERTO URREA'S NOVEL *THE HUMMINGBIRD'S DAUGHTER* (2005)

At the turn of the nineteenth century, stories of Teresa Urrea, also known as "La Santa de Cabora," had tremendous resonance along the US-Mexico borderlands. These stories consisted of a teenaged curandera, a faith healer that would heal anyone who would come to her father's hacienda in Cabora, Sonora, creating large gatherings seeking healing and hope. Described in newspapers of the time as large *romerías*, these gatherings consisted of people from all walks of life would come to seek healing from the girl who purportedly rose from the dead and gained healing powers from God.[1] Teresa Urrea was an agent of change in her historical context with her message of dignity for all and denunciations against those who loved power and money. Among her many followers were the Yaqui and Mayo people, two Indigenous groups who were constantly threatened by Spanish and Mexican colonialist efforts to displace and kill them to take their ancestral homelands. Teresa's devotees spurred political dissension in her name as she became a transnational religious icon during this time period.

Paul J. Vanderwood writes in his book *The Power of God against the Guns of Government* that devotees of Teresa Urrea fought against the Mexican military in the Tomochic Rebellion of 1891–1892 in her name. This ultimately led to President Porfirio Díaz exiling Teresa Urrea and her father Tomás Urrea to the United States in 1892.[2] She died in 1906 in Clifton, Arizona, and in the years after her death, there were various literary representations of Teresa Urrea's life and work. These include American historian William Curry

Holden's 1978 biography titled *Teresita* and Mexican author Brianda Domecq's 1998 novel *La insólita historia de la Santa de Cabora*. However, Luis Alberto Urrea's novel *The Hummingbird's Daughter*, published in 2005, stands out among these writings because he is Teresa Urrea's great-great-grandnephew and a Chicano writer from the US-Mexico borderlands. For Luis Alberto Urrea, this project of writing a novel on the life of Teresa Urrea was the result of twenty years of research of a historical transnational figure that was also his relative who lived over one hundred years ago. Urrea's work brings about interesting questions of transnationalism, faith, protest, and nation-building.

Luis Alberto Urrea's *The Hummingbird's Daughter* is a retelling of his great aunt's life and her historicopolitical context. Teresa Urrea's story is located within the historical context of late nineteenth-century transnational space of the US-Mexico borderlands in which resistance to the colonialism of the Mexican government was inspired by spirituality in the Yaquis and Mayos, leading to uprisings. This novel represents the violence inherent in perceptions of the US-Mexico borderlands as a violent space due to the existence of Indigenous communities, such as the Yaquis, that are resistant to colonialism. Johan Galtung discusses violence that is physical and violence that is psychological, both of which are manifested in the treatment of the Yaqui and Mayo people by the Mexican government, as well as the exiling of Teresa Urrea. The physical violence and psychological violence historically inflicted on these Indigenous groups, which is also represented in the novel, are "violence that works on the body, and violence that works on the soul," respectively.[3] Mexico's nation-building efforts that included the removal of the Yaquis and Mayos from their ancestral lands were both physical violence on their bodies and psychological violence through continual threats through military presence throughout the borderlands region and the exile of Teresa Urrea. Additionally, the Catholic Church was guilty of involvement through their reporting of "rebellious behavior" among these Indigenous groups, as will be discussed in this chapter.

The historical Teresa Urrea was a threat to nation-building efforts of Mexico because of her positionality as a woman, a curandera, and a faith leader on the borderlands, and Luis Alberto Urrea represents this threat through the character of Teresa Urrea in his novel in the way hegemonies react to her healing ministry and her followers. Historically and culturally, Teresa Urrea is an agent of borderlands consciousness, in which her faith healing practices brought to impoverished and oppressed communities in her region the awareness of how to resist an imperialist government through the dignity of spirituality.

Teresa Urrea, a Historical Religious Icon

Teresa Urrea, the historical figure, was a healer in Cabora, Sonora, who also spoke out against the oppression of Indigenous people that were suffering at the hands of hacendados and the Mexican military. Desireé A. Martín describes Teresa Urrea in the following passage:

> Teresa Urrea is at once a popular borderlands saint, a faith healer, a literary representation, a catalyst for indigenous and peasant rebellion, a regional legend, a subject of historical research, a media darling, a performer, a celebrity, a loving daughter and mother, a feminist icon, an "early Chicana," a symbol of transnational borderlands identity, a determined self-promoter, a hero to the poor, infirm, and dispossessed.[4]

Teresa Urrea was born in 1873 in Sinaloa, Mexico, to an Indigenous young mother named Cayetana, who was a servant, and fathered by the hacendado Tomás Urrea. According to Vanderwood, Tomás Urrea came from a very influential and wealthy family since colonial times in Mexico, a family who had also produced governmental leaders in Sinaloa and Sonora in the nineteenth century.[5] However, that power would soon be challenged: after supporting a gubernatorial candidate who opposed Porfirio Díaz and lost the election, Tomás

Urrea found himself fleeing Sinaloa and settling in Cabora, Sonora. It was then, when Teresa reached her teens, that Tomás accepted her as his daughter and allowed her to live in his home. Most accounts indicate that after Teresa was accepted by her father, she became ill. There are a variety of accounts of what her illness consisted of: Vanderwood postulates that she had convulsions for thirteen days, and after awakening from a trance she "lingered in a daze that periodically deepened into a trance" for three months.[6] There are also varied accounts of what caused the illness: they included epilepsy, finding the man she loved with another woman, and a man raping her.[7] When Teresa healed from these convulsion episodes, she was reportedly able to heal people.

This is an important turning point in the accounts of Teresa Urrea's life. Jennifer Koshatka Seman explains that Teresa Urrea's healing powers came about after a very traumatic experience that would have possibly left her for dead, a common theme in the stories of curanderos: "many curanderos undergo a kind of symbolic death and rebirth."[8] Soon after healing from her convulsions, Teresa Urrea began healing people, and the word spread quickly throughout the region of the girl in Cabora with divine powers to cure disease, wounds, and many other ailments that people suffered. As people gathered around her home to find healing, they also heard the sermons she gave, filled with liberatory theological principles of justice and God's love for the oppressed.[9]

While Teresa Urrea was an ally and supporter of the Yaqui and Mayo people in their fight for their land, historians have argued that she may not have been the outspoken activist that is represented in *The Hummingbird's Daughter*. And while this may be historical fact, it is also true that she became a transnational religious icon embraced by many who, in their fight for their dignity, rebelled against the Mexican government. Vanderwood explains in his article titled "Santa Teresa: Mexico's Joan of Arc" that Teresa Urrea became a symbol of hope and dignity for the fight for their land, so much so that Díaz decided to exile her to the United States rather than execute her:

> The crafty old dictator probably recognized that the greatest threat to his government would be from a mass rebellion of the poor and disadvantaged, and from an individual such as Teresa Urrea who could inspire such a revolt. He also may have realized that his killing or imprisoning Teresa would make her even more dangerous as a martyr.[10]

Vanderwood also explains that Teresa Urrea sympathized with the Yaquis but "never led the Yaquis to battles."[11] However, this was enough for the Díaz regime to exile her and her father to the United States, and the way she was exiled demonstrates how hegemonies in Mexico City and US railroad companies worked together continuously in oppressive and violent efforts to displace Indigenous people and those in poverty along the US-Mexico borderlands, as will be discussed later in this chapter.

As a political exile, Teresa Urrea's life was that of a transnational political figure, which needs to be situated in the transnational history of the US-Mexico borderlands, or what Ramón A. Gutiérrez and Elliott Young call "transnationalizing borderlands history"—that is, a reimagining of how to study the US-Mexico borderlands' history by taking into account that this space is not a periphery, that there is no edge to it, and that the space rather encapsulates the histories of both sides of the border.[12] In conceptualizing the borderlands as a transnational space rather than a periphery, a consciousness comes forth that is decolonial, as Emma Pérez explains: "the borderlands are also the interstices where the decolonial imaginary glides to introduce the possibility of a postcolonial, postnational consciousness."[13] The cultural knowledge of the story of Teresa Urrea is a not just postcolonial and postnational but also generative of a borderlands consciousness: it gives the borderlands community the ability to see the power of spiritual dignity and celebrates the revolutionary acts of the Yaqui and Mayo people that resisted colonization.

Teresa Urrea lived in a time period that followed nearly half a century of internal conflict in Mexico, as well as invasions by powerful foreign actors. Díaz took power in Mexico in 1876, starting the three-decade dictatorship known as the Porfiriato. It is during this time that Díaz embarked on his modernization project of Mexico while at the same time molding a Mexican national identity centered on the idea of *mestizaje*: a racialized Mexican national identity that claims an oppressed positionality as children of a violent conquest of the Spanish over the *indígena* and was claimed to be embraced by Mexicans. The liberal Mexican government that resulted after the reform laws were put in place in 1863 created the idea of mestizaje, but this racial identity project ignored the existence and dignity of Indigenous groups and persons of African descent in Mexico. These efforts were even stronger after the Mexican Revolution of 1910–1920, with the term *la raza cósmica*, coined by José Vasconcelos in 1925, denoting a Pan-American race, a fifth race as a result of the mixing of races from the conquest.[14]

The conceptualization of this futuristic race, an ultimate mestizaje of sorts, has been used as a nation-building tool in Mexico: "the celebration of the superiority of a mixed Latin America over a North America hell-bent on maintaining a vicious racial purity made it easy for elites to deny the racism of Mexican society."[15] This idea of a utopian fifth race, or what is conceptualized as mestizaje, is a transnational ideology erasing Indigenous persons as well as persons of African descent while also justifying violence against them; thus, mestizaje cannot be disentangled from setter colonialism. This endeavor of creating a national identity was at the fore of the government's efforts and went hand in hand with the terrorizing and attempts to colonize territories of the Yaqui and Mayo people in Sonora.

The Hummingbird's Daughter is a Chicano literary piece that denounces violence against the Yaqui and Mayo people in Mexico by emphasizing Teresa Urrea's undying support and love for the Yaquis and Mayos. The violence perpetuated by the government in the name of nation-building is an important theme in *The Hummingbird's Daughter*: the protagonist Teresa Urrea gains a platform through her healing abilities, and she uses it to denounce the oppression executed by the Mexican government on the Yaquis and Mayos. She ultimately becomes a transnational religious icon that the Yaquis and Mayos embrace in their rebellion against the Mexican government because of her faith healing and spiritual message of dignity.

The Story of Teresa Urrea: Written Words of Dignity

The Hummingbird's Daughter is divided into five sections, or books, that highlight the timeline of Teresa Urrea's life in Mexico: the birth and childhood of Teresa Urrea; the move of the Urrea ranch from Ocoroni, Sinaloa, to Cabora, Sonora; the perspective of the Urreas regarding the pacification of the Yaquis; the coma and healing powers of Teresa Urrea; and the flight of Teresa Urrea and her father after threats against their lives. Each book presents the development of the person of Teresa Urrea: from apprenticeship with Huila in book 1 to her ministry of healing and political dissent in book 4. Additionally, in this novel an important detail about Teresa Urrea's life is that she learns to read and write. The emphasis that *Hummingbird's Daughter* places on Teresa Urrea learning to read and write is significant to study because Luis Alberto Urrea implies that Teresa Urrea may have written some autobiographical pieces. In the author's note at the end of the novel, Luis Alberto Urrea claims, "Lauro Aguirre's *Tomóchic!* (also known by different titles) is interesting, since it suggests it was edited—if not co-written—by Teresita herself."[16] In bringing this claim to light, Luis Alberto Urrea makes a valid interrogation of the portrayal of Teresa Urrea throughout the last century as a young Mexican borderlands woman who was illiterate.

While there is much evidence of a great religious following from Teresa's healing ministry, there is not a consensus on whether she was literate. Vanderwood asserts she "had no formal education, but taught herself to read and write, if only in the most rudimentary way; she could write her name but not much more, and her reading was limited to the simplest of texts."[17] However, in *The*

Hummingbird's Daughter, Luis Alberto Urrea presents a Teresa Urrea that is literate, as scholars such as Amy Robinson would argue is true. Robinson writes about the significance of Teresa Urrea's literacy, indicating that this portrayal is central to her effectiveness as a political dissenter, describing "Teresa's ability to read, write and publish as a key to her transformation from private healer to public threat."[18] She goes on to prove this point by stating that literacy is "compatible with her qualities as a woman who actively and aggressively defied the male-dominated parameters of her existence by forging a public and political identity from the private domain of her bodily and spiritual talents."[19] It is clear that her words, whether written or spoken, carried immense power. As Robinson asserts, Luis Alberto Urrea presents to the reader a Teresa Urrea that is not only literate but powerful in her language of protest. In *The Hummingbird's Daughter*, Porfirio Díaz learns of Teresa Urrea not by word of mouth but by her own words in a news article that reaches him through Lauro Aguirre's newspaper.[20] The presentation of Teresa Urrea as a faith leader who was a political activist in *The Hummingbird's Daughter* is an interesting and opposing portrayal of Vanderwood's presentation of a meek Teresa Urrea that is interested not in politics but rather in spiritual matters.[21]

Aguirre is the historical figure, as well as literary character, in Teresa Urrea's story that brings literacy into her life. Tomás Urrea established a friendship with Aguirre, an engineer and an ardent anti-Porfirian journalist, when the latter visited Cabora after hearing about Teresa's miracles. In 1892, Aguirre wrote about Teresa in his newspaper, *El Independiente*, which was situated in Nogales, Arizona. The power of the written word reached many because other newspapers wrote about her healing powers as well.[22] As early as 1896, the El Paso newspaper *Daily Herald* printed several stories on Teresa Urrea, and she became a media sensation. Teresa's fame grew to a transnational audience, and her influence also spread due to the written word.

In the novel, Luis Alberto Urrea fictionalizes the media exposure by representing nationwide exposure of Teresa Urrea's healing powers that reach Díaz. In this fictional narrative, Díaz sends a group of reporters to Cabora after reading the article by Teresa Urrea. A comical incident involves Tomás Urrea, who is not a believer in his daughter's gift at this point, and a bald reporter: he tells the bald reporter that if Teresa Urrea is indeed a saint, then hair would grow on his head. After witnessing the miracles, the reporter approaches Tomás: "he only bent toward the patron and rubbed the peach fuzz that had appeared on his head and laughed."[23] The reporters write their articles that reach the presidential palace in Mexico City:

> When they wrote their articles, they alarmed President Díaz further by extolling her virtues, reporting miracles performed in their presence, and suggesting that the government attend to native rights in the issue of the land thievery and genocide currently taking place along the Río Maya and Río Yaqui valleys.[24]

Both historically and in the novel, the message of Teresa Urrea was heard about across Mexico, which was proving to be effective in her message proclaiming the dignity of the Yaqui and Mayo people. In the novel, the written word is significant because of the spread of the influence of Teresa Urrea to powerful government officials, and the spoken word is what made Teresa Urrea famous in the US-Mexico borderlands. While powerful actors were located in Mexico City, their eyes were on the borderlands, feeling nervous at the possibility of uprisings that could threaten the nation-building efforts of the Mexican federal government. Díaz's government had eyes and ears on the ground in Cabora, and in *The Hummingbird's Daughter*, these eyes and ears come in the form of Father Gastélum.

Teresa Urrea and the Catholic Church

Father Gastélum is another historical figure that is fictionalized in Luis Alberto Urrea's *The Hummingbird's Daughter*. Holden writes in *Teresita* that "the most vehement among the anti-Teresa priests was

Father Manuel Gustelúm of Uranchic."[25] Although there is a difference in spelling in the name of the historical priest (Gustelúm) and the literary representation of the priest (Gastélum), it is indeed the same Catholic priest that sought the downfall of Teresa Urrea. He was the local priest of the region that Teresa inhabited, and in the novel he has connections to the Porfirian government and is essentially a spy. In the novel, Teresa Urrea gives sermons on her porch to the crowd of people seeking healing, and her devotees who listen to them then spread her message all through Sonora, Chihuahua, Arizona, New Mexico, and Texas. These sermons in the novel are short but powerful, denouncing hegemonies like the Porfirian regime and the Catholic Church. In one sermon, Teresa angers Father Gastélum, in her challenge of religiosity while exalting the act of love: "'For God,' she preached from her porch, 'religions are nothing, signify nothing.'"[26] She calls for the masses to love and do good, angering Gastélum to the point of demanding that Teresa explain the role of the Church, and so she goes on to critique the dynamics between a priest and his church:

> "Priests love because they are ordered to love."
> "How dare you! I don't need Rome to tell me how to love."[27]

In this passage from the novel, Teresa Urrea challenges the Church in their theology of love by declaring that they love out of obligation and calls for a greater and more difficult love: the one that upholds, respects, and celebrates the humanity of your fellow human being. The fact that she differentiates this type of love from the obligatory love of the clergy sends the message to the masses that the Church does not see their humanity but rather seeks to exploit them.

The public exchange between Teresa Urrea and Father Gastélum in the novel leads the Indigenous people that have visited Teresa Urrea, such as those who led the Tomochic Uprising of 1892, the Tigers of Tomóchic and their leader Cruz Chávez, who calls himself the "Pope of Mexico," to become devoted followers of her messages. Teresa Urrea's relationships to Indigenous historical figures such as Cruz Chávez are significant in this narrative. Luis Alberto Urrea writes this same group as present at Teresa Urrea's sermon on political dissent:

> "Do you believe God put your feet on this land? God gave land to every man and woman! And this is your land! This land is holy! *Do you believe?*"
>
> *Yes! We believe!*
>
> "These octopi strangle you with their sinful arms. Greed! Greed is a sin! No man, whether he is white or brown, can take the land from you! It came from God! Only God may take it away from you!
>
> "Tell me now! DO YOU BELIEVE?"
>
> They had yelled her name, They had danced. They had lifted their hands and fallen to the ground.
>
> She had smiled.
>
> "This is not a call to war," the Pope of Mexico said.
>
> "It is to us," his men said.[28]

In the novel, the people declare her a saint, and she makes use of her positionality to send the message of protest against a regime that is actively and violently displacing Indigenous people of that region. Just as she did in the sermon criticizing the Church, the novel's Teresa Urrea dichotomizes the sovereignty of God and the authority of the Mexican government. In doing so, the persons present at her sermon understand that whatever laws and policies the Porfirian regime puts in place, if it disrespects the land sovereignty of the Indigenous people to whom, according to Teresa Urrea, God has given the land, then that government is outside the will of God. The rhetorical question Teresa Urrea posed was, Who or what earthly power can overpower God himself? The sovereignty of Indigenous people *is* within the will of the almighty God, and this message is empowering for many of her devotees to continue their struggle against a sinful, greedy government, with the blessing of God.

However, historically the Roman Catholic Church colluded with the Mexican government. Vanderwood describes the Porfiriato as a time that valued the veneer of peace in Mexican society and sought the "aura of the Church as peacekeeper."[29] Robert D. Conger wrote a dissertation on this topic and explains:

> The church hierarchy was disposed to cooperate with Díaz after the defeat of the monarchy it had supported and the recent persecutions under the Lerdo de Tejada regime. A truce period seemed highly desirable, and cooperation offered the possibility of regaining its lost prestige and even some of its power.[30]

Because of the efforts on behalf of the Catholic Church to gain some power in Mexico, their cooperation was effective in having clergy report to the Díaz regime about the state of their respective regions. In *The Hummingbird's Daughter*, the character of Father Gastélum declares himself the eyes and ears of the Vatican as well as pledges allegiance to the "second father . . . in Mexico City"—that is, Porfirio Díaz—in a tense exchange with Aguirre. Gastélum warns Aguirre that he writes reports to "our leader" and makes the claim that he "[serves] only God . . . and the republic."[31] Throughout the novel, Father Gastélum turns into a type of metonymy for the Porfiriato because of his fervent servanthood to his "second father." He uses his positionality as a priest to go around Northern Mexico to rebuke Indigenous groups for following Teresa Urrea, all while also cutting backroom dealings with powerful actors such as Governor Lauro Carillo of Chihuahua to steal paintings from the Tomochic church that the Indigenous people regard as sacred. He sends these as a gift to the wife of Díaz to win the president's favor.[32]

It is important to emphasize the juxtaposition of Father Gastélum and Teresa Urrea in their declarations of being servants of God. In the novel, Father Gastélum's second father is Díaz while Teresa Urrea is preaching scathing anti-Díaz sermons daily. Gastélum's servanthood to Díaz consists of "watching her for irregularities and heresies. She did not disappoint him—when she began to preach against priests, he turned crimson and scribbled in his notebook."[33] Her use of the same religious rhetoric of servanthood to God puts her on the same authoritative standing as Father Gastélum. This is significant in a transnational lens due to the fact that Gastélum was given authority over the borderlands region, once again representing how centering of the borderlands was crucial in the nation building efforts of Díaz. Holden indicates that it was Gustelúm who "immediately dispatched a runner to Chihuahua City with a message to the governor stating that the people of Tomochic were in a state of revolt."[34] The Mexican government needed the eyes and ears of the Church to have control of this territory to attain his goal of a modern Mexico at all costs.

The Yaqui Pacification Program

Understanding the Porfirian efforts of nation-building in the late nineteenth century is vital to the discussion of the representation in *The Hummingbird's Daughter* of the brutality that the Yaquis and Mayos faced historically. Díaz's desperation to control the lands of the Yaqui and Mayo demonstrates the importance of the borderlands in the mission to build a desired imagined community of a Mexican nation, the mestizaje that erases Indigenous people. Díaz and his government had the influence and the political connections with powerful actors, both domestic and foreign, to attain the goal of modernizing Mexico and profiting from taking land from the Yaquis and Mayos to hand over to American companies. The relationship between the Mexican government and the US government was not equitable, but that didn't stop Díaz from demanding that there be deportation policies in place in the United States in order to suppress the fleeing Yaquis into Arizona. Before 1908, there was not much done to deport Yaqui refugees back to Mexico. And when they fled, Arizona was a place of refuge for them as well as an opportunity to purchase arms and weapons for the resistance back in Sonora. However, Evelyn Hu-Dehart explains that a financial crisis in the United States in November 1907 led its government to start deportation and border-policing policies, heeding the calls of Díaz to address the migratory flow of Yaquis into the United States.[35] The most lucrative business dealings with Mexico were the building of railroads into Guaymas, Sonora, and these were severely affected by the financial crisis of November 1907. And while it may seem that the United States had a passive role in the violence perpetuated against the Yaquis and Mayos, they were very much involved in the perpetuation of the *indio bárbaro* portrayal of "violent" Indigenous people resisting colonization of their lands. María Josefina Saldaña-Portillo explains how the indio bárbaro stereotype was used as justification of violence against Indigenous groups on both sides of the US-Mexico border:

> The nineteenth century ushered in a Mexican liberal nationalism premised on a mestizo model of abstract political emancipation that was broadly inclusive in terms of race. The exception to this racial inclusion was the indio bárbaro who in fact enabled the Mexican demos to come together in racial unity through the practices of scalping and beheading. Over the course of the liberal nineteenth century, the iteration of the indio bárbaro lost its colonial fluidity, ceased to be the potential economic and political ally, and instead became all that must be pushed out of the nation's borders. Mexico and the United States colluded in producing this iteration of the indio bárbaro through the transnational scalping posses and through the Treaty of Guadalupe Hidalgo (TGH), which brokered peace at the expense of the tribus salvajes.[36]

The federal Mexican government colluded internally as well with state government officials and hacendados "with prestige, such as the Maytorenas, and those with good government contracts, such as Aureliano Torres."[37] If the Yaquis were deemed useful in Sonora by these government officials, the rich hacendados, and American companies, then arrangements were made to utilize Yaquis during the 1908 deportations. One example Hu-Dehart gives is Aureliano Torres, who "was temporarily loaned twenty-five Yaquis from the penitentiary in Guaymas during the height of the deportation in June to help him harvest his chick peas."[38] The Maytorena family was also given workers from the penitentiary to address the labor needs for their agricultural production. In efforts to utilize all resources, including labor of incarcerated persons, the Mexican government ensured that industries such as agriculture continued to produce.

Additionally, there was collusion within the Díaz administration. Hu-Dehart explains that Diaz's secretary of development, colonization and industry, Olegario Molina "was also the biggest henequen *hacendado* in Yucatán. Also, in his official capacity, he was granting some of the most generous concessions in Sonora, specifically in the Yaqui Valley, to such interests as the Richardson Construction Company."[39] This was a blatant conflict of interest that served the enrichment of Molina as well as American companies such as Richardson Construction Company that were "interested mainly in agriculturally developing the Yaqui Valley through colonization and irrigation."[40] The forced imported labor force comprised of enslaved Yaquis permitted the henequen industry of Yucatán to flourish as the global exports of henequen increased during this time period. The euphemistic justification by the Mexican government of this violent displacement of an entire group of people is that it was actually a display of benevolence, once again invoking the indio bárbaro stereotype to the benefit of the rich and privileged and to the despair of the Indigenous groups resisting colonization. Additionally, Díaz himself signed off on the displacement and enslavement of the Yaquis after Alberto Cubillas, who was the secretary of the state government, "expressed his opinion to Ramón Corral that only the complete deportation of the tribe could solve the rebel problem. Corral wired back that both he and the President approved of the decision to deport all Yaquis."[41] The collusion of the cabinet members of Díaz's administration was a disgraceful effort to euphemize and legally justify the removal of Yaquis from their homeland and their genocide.

Díaz's oppressive regime had a tight reign over the entire country and had its eye particularly in the Río Yaqui Valley in Sonora, located in Northern Mexico. The Yaquis have resisted colonization since the days of the Spanish Empire, therefore their resistance to Porfirian efforts of pacification were always existent despite the rise and fall of leaders of the resistance. While many were rebels involved in resistance efforts, many Yaquis sought to work on haciendas, mines, and railroads with the goal of leading a quiet life. The Mexican government demanded that all Yaquis undergo registration for passports as a way to control them. If they did not have a passport, they were arrested and deemed rebels. This is but one example of Laura Pulido's discussion on nation-building settler colonialism in which Indigenous groups were required to pacify and mold into the mestizo Mexican national identity.[42]

The pacification project of the Yaquis came to a head in the years 1904–1907, according to Hu-Dehart. She describes the ruthlessness of the Mexican government toward the Yaquis in the following passage:

> The slightest suspicion came to constitute sufficient grounds for arrest. Sometimes, the *yaquería* of a whole hacienda, ranch, or mine which the rebels had just raided were rounded up for deportation on charges of collusion with the enemy. Increasingly the orders called for arrests of Yaquis "with all their families, so that not a single Yaqui remains, neither big nor small."[43]

The threat of deportation was a reality for the Yaqui, whether they cooperated with the government or not. Nicole Guidotti-Hernández explains that US "railroad and farming companies with venture capital" sought to enter the Río Yaqui Valley, efforts that fit nicely into Díaz's modernization project.[44] The resistance of the Yaquis to abide by these modernization efforts were to be met with brute force. While the Mexican government's renewed campaign at the end of the nineteenth century to subjugate Yaquis started in the 1890s, 1908 turned out to be the most devastating year due to the indiscriminate deportation of men, women, and children to Yucatán. There are not official numbers on the displacement of Yaquis during this so-called pacification program. Hu-Dehart indicates that "in [Governor] Izábal's 1903–1907 report to the State Congress, he listed some 2,000 Yaquis forced to 'leave the territory,' and another 600 captives freed for informing on their fellows."[45]

Luis Alberto Urrea writes in *The Hummingbird's Daughter* that the Mexican military "collected Yaquis from unprotected villages and herded them toward the sea. No one knew where they went—whole families vanished overnight."[46] In the novel, Tomás Urrea is sure these stories are true given that he encounters an old friend one day, Captain Enriquez. Tomás rides out into Yaqui territory after banishing his estranged wife, Loreto, from his property and runs into Mexican soldiers with a group of Yaqui prisoners. Tomás feels the confidence to approach the soldiers because Enriquez is an old friend:

> "What is this?" Tomás asked.
> "Bad business," Enriquez said. "Bad business."
> "Where are you taking them?"
> "It is better not to ask."
> Tomás watched the tired Yaquis shuffle away.
> "And their land?" he asked.
> Enriquez repeated: "Bad business, my friend."[47]

Tomás soon realizes that another horseman is carrying scalped heads of Yaquis. He displays disgust and shock, to which his friend Captain Enriquez advises, "Go home, Tomás. This is a bad business, and you don't belong here. . . . Go home. Lock your gates."[48] The terror of what Tomás has witnessed stays with him, and throughout the rest of the novel he is one of the few characters that confront Teresa regarding the real dangers of angering the Mexican government.

Exiling of Teresa Urrea in Partnership with the Neighbors of the North

The exiling of Teresa and Tomás Urrea demonstrates the transnational importance of the US-Mexico borderlands and the efforts of settler colonialism by the Porfirian regime. When Díaz exiles Teresa and Tomás Urrea in *The Hummingbird's Daughter*, they are forced onto a train that takes them to Nogales, Arizona. Luis Alberto Urrea inserts a detail in the novel that signals the transnational centrality of the US-Mexico borderlands. In Guaymas, Teresa and her father are jailed awaiting their sentence, which they thought would be death, yet as they are taken to the lieutenant to hear their sentence, Teresa and Tomás Urrea learn that they are in fact going to be exiled:

> "Due to the immense generosity of General Díaz and the Mexican government, the sentence of death will forthwith commuted to expulsion..."
> "Wait. We are being deported?" Tomás said.
> The lieutenant gestured at the train.
> "Mexico's newest rail line is at your disposal. As you can see, it is a Santa Fe train. Mexico railroads are in partnership with the Santa Fe line, and this rolling stock has come to us from—"
> "Wait!" Tomás said.
> "Yes?"
> "Exiled?"
> "Not to return. I would consider that a good offer."[49]

Luis Alberto Urrea represents the transnational relationships between the Mexican government and US railroad companies through the mention that the Santa Fe rail line will be taking Teresa and Tomás Urrea to their destination in the United States. The Santa Fe rail line was an American line that traveled as far north as Minnesota and Chicago, and its southernmost point was Guaymas, Sonora. US railroad companies sought the opportunity to build a railroad into Mexico for the trading that could bring about a lucrative global market.

In fact, Consuelo Boyd explains that the Sonora Railway, as it came to be named, took over twenty years to complete due to resistance by the people of Sonora, especially by the Yaquis and Mayos. It was Governor Ignacio Pesqueira who pushed for the railroad to be built to "[settle] border problems with the United States and [attract] American investors to Mexico.... [He sought] economic ties with the United States."[50] The settler colonialist mindset of both the Mexican government as well as US companies was what Pulido calls "overlapping Mexican and US racial formations and nation-building projects":

> These formations are both sequential and spatially and temporally overlapping. Here, we must draw on our most sophisticated understandings of place—how to understand a region as a palimpsest, a border zone, and a boundary simultaneously? While Mexico incorporated indigeneity into its nation-building efforts, mestizaje has been highly contradictory. In contrast, the US sought to obliterate native people physically and forged a white racial and national identity exclusive of them. Consequently, in the US, native peoples are seen as distinct from the larger nation and insist they are sovereign.[51]

Even Boyd's essay on the history of the Guaymas railroad is full of racial assertions of Indigenous groups being obstacles to nation-building efforts. Both countries needed to create their national identities and the point of departure has always been the US-Mexico border. Therefore, efforts at establishing economic ties through the building of an expensive and invasive project like a railroad helped both nation-states develop the very notions that Pulido discusses in the above quote. Thus, in the passage from the novel of Teresa Urrea's expulsion being carried out with a US rail line, Luis Alberto Urrea exposes the reader to a borderlands consciousness in the collusion of the Mexican government and a US railroad company to exile a political leader such as Teresa Urrea who helped influence a Yaqui and Mayo uprising.

Conclusion

Guidotti-Hernández rightfully assesses that Díaz was obsessed with modernity. After the Mexican nation-state's bloody Reform War, the invasion of the French, and the loss of the northern territories,

Díaz's goal was to build a nation that was modern, strong, and self-sufficient. However, the Indigenous people who resisted these nation-building efforts were killed, enslaved, and violated. And the wealthy looked at the modernization project of Mexico, including the Indigenous genocide and displacement, and approved: "The ruling classes and intellectuals embraced positivism at this time not only as an intellectual trend but also as a justification for big landowners to add to their territories the lands of indigenous peoples."[52] Evidently, the Yaquis' and Mayos' resistance to these ideologies of land ownership led to the violent and genocidal campaign to displace them.

Toward the end of *The Hummingbird's Daughter*, Cruz Chávez asks Teresa Urrea what she thinks her purpose on earth is. She answers: "'Love for God, love for each other. Reconciliation. Service.' She poked him with a finger. 'Joy!'"[53] Cruz chastises her for this, telling her that there are armed riders that find joy in killing people, which leads to a theological discussion on whether or not God allows suffering in the ailing communities seeking healing:

> "Tell me which is worse, Pope Chávez—is it that God *cannot* cure them all, or that He *will not* cure them?"
>
> Cruz was silent. He had no answer. He resented the question.
>
> "This," she said, "is what I live with."
>
> He shrugged.
>
> "You should know the answer," she said. "You should know what it is you really think of God."
>
> She got up from her seat.
>
> "Then," she continued, "you should decide why the president of Mexico does not help these people."[54]

Luis Alberto Urrea's representation of Teresa Urrea represents violent hegemonies and through a theological lens brings about the argument again and again that all people deserve dignity: a dignity that comes with the right to life, land, and well-being, a dignity that encapsulates borderlands consciousness. As discussed in this chapter, the historical Teresa Urrea was a powerful transnational religious icon that represented for many this dignity as they faced oppressive and violent threats against that very dignity. At the end of that same conversation with Cruz, Teresa says to him, "'God likes tools,' she said. 'You and I, we are the tools of God. We cannot afford to rust or break. Do you see?'"[55] A teenaged woman in a rural town of Sonora was this borderlands tool, who claimed that the divine will of God is that all have dignity and that the land belonged to the Yaqui and Mayo people, and for this message she was deemed a dangerous threat by the authorities of the Mexican government. Through Teresa Urrea's message to her Yaqui and Mayo followers to believe that the land is theirs because it was given to them by God himself, Teresa Urrea directly challenged the racist efforts of settler colonialism of the Mexican government, as well as the encroachment of the US government and the companies owned by North Americans. Her name will always go down in history as a battle cry, a borderlands consciousness of her devotees, brave Yaquis, Mayos, and poor people along the US-Mexico transnational borderlands.

CHAPTER TWO

CAPITALISM AND COMPLICITY BETWEEN THE US GOVERNMENT AND RAILROAD CORPORATIONS ALONG THE US-MEXICO BORDERLANDS

In 2004, the *Los Angeles Times* published an article about Modesta Avila, a Mexican American woman in California who in 1889 became "Orange County's first convicted felon" by rebelling against two of the era's most powerful and wealthy entities: the railroad industry and the US government. In an act of protest against the Santa Fe Railroad, which she claimed was noisy, disruptive, and built on her property without her consent, Avila hung her clothesline across the tracks near her home. She was convicted of "obstructing a railroad right-of-way" and, at twenty-two years of age, sentenced to three years at San Quentin State Prison. Avila died of a fever just two years later.[1]

    This utter cruelty in response to a nonviolent and essentially harmless act of protest reflects the violence that railroad companies inflicted upon local communities in the nineteenth and early twentieth centuries, the complicity of the US government, and the impunity they both enjoyed in the process. Avila lived during a period of rapid industrialization in the United States, and as heads of what some would call America's first big business and one of the nation's most lucrative industries, railroad tycoons acquired an immense amount of wealth and power. The history of railway construction in the nineteenth century and into the twentieth reveals ongoing cooperation between railroad corporations and the US government, each committed to violent nation-building efforts that relied on westward expansion, white supremacy, and capitalist growth. Central to these efforts was establishing and preserving the imagined community of a nation—a vision of an ideal US citizenry that was rich, white, and male. Only members of this exclusive club would be allowed land, safety, wealth, and free rein to pursue them. People like Avila threatened this imagined community with their mere existence. Indeed, the United States' conceptualization of ideal citizens, an imagined community of a nation, was always drawn along racial and class lines, and strongly tied to land acquisition. The ideology and mythology of manifest destiny—the belief that US westward expansion was God's will—had a stronghold in the nineteenth century. This settler-colonialist nation-building project was used to justify the displacement, impoverishment, and exploitation of nonwhite populations across North America.

This chapter analyzes the structural violence inherent in nineteenth- and early twentieth-century railroad construction along the US-Mexico borderlands, as the US government actively provided resources like funding and legislation to benefit railroad companies and their stakeholders—the wealthiest people in the country. In service to a nation-building project to further enrich this imagined community of a nation comprised of affluent white men, this state support allowed the railroad industry to inflict violence in the form of exploitation, discrimination, criminalization, theft, and even death against nonwhite communities across the US-Mexico borderlands.

Mexican Americans exposed and denounced these abuses, including the US government's complicity, through their cultural production, particularly literary representations. In this chapter, I consider two novels: *The Squatter and the Don: A Novel Descriptive of Contemporary Occurrences in California* by María Amparo Ruiz de Burton (1885) and *Las aventuras de Don Chipote; o, Cuando los pericos mamen* (*The Adventures of Don Chipote; or, When Parrots Breast-Feed*) by Daniel Venegas (1928). Both works provide representations of railroad companies actively impoverishing entire communities and mistreating Mexican immigrant laborers who laid the tracks throughout the US-Mexico borderlands. Keenly aware of these abuses, the authors wrote these stories as cautionary tales but also as public denunciations of the violence inflicted upon themselves and their communities. Both authors embedded their censure in their narratives and addressed their audience directly to expose this structural violence and incite action. These are protest novels, works of literary activism produced by the people of the US-Mexico borderlands.

"Public" Domain: US Expansion, Land Rights, and the Railroad Industry

The United States expanded tremendously in the mid-nineteenth century, the belief in manifest destiny pushing the country westward, ultimately taking Mexican lands, and continuing a nation-building project in which settler colonialism was at the root. Many Anglo-American settlers came into Texas in the early nineteenth century assuring the Mexican government they would respect Mexican sovereignty, including antislavery laws. However, these settlers fomented resistance against the Mexican government, leading to armed conflict and ultimately secession from Mexico. Texas declared independence from Mexico in 1836, and after starting as its own nation-state, it then officially became a US state in 1846. Soon after, disputes over the US-Mexico border led to armed conflict between the United States and Mexico. When the Mexican-American War ended in 1848, Mexico had lost almost one-third of its territory to the United States, which more than doubled in size with the addition of what would become the states of California, Utah, Nevada, Arizona, and New Mexico, as well as parts of Colorado, Oklahoma, Kansas, and Wyoming. California gained statehood just two years later in 1850.

The acquisition of this vast expanse of land meant that Mexican nationals were now living in territories that belonged to the United States. Although the Treaty of Guadalupe Hidalgo had "specifically promised full and complete protection of all property rights of Mexicans," Congress passed the California Land Act of 1851 to determine land ownership in these territories. The law "threw the burden of proof on every Californian who claimed land" and created the Public Land Commission, a three-person committee tasked with examining deeds from landowners who had inhabited California before the cession in 1848.[2] However, the commissioners, Redick McKee, G. W. Barbour, and O. M. Wozencraft, denied many Mexican Californios' land claims. This was mostly due to differences in legal definitions of ownership since some of the land was owned by communities and some by individuals. Likewise, documentation in the Spanish and Mexican legal systems was more community-based and therefore their conceptualization of land was in relation to the community. The US legal system, on the other hand, "viewed the earth's surface as an imaginary grid laid out on a piece of paper, and cartography and surveying were used to identify physical features of a particular parcel."[3] Since the 1851 law stipulated that all rejected claims would "within two years . . . be considered as part of the public domain of the United States," the US government took ownership of Mexican Californios' lands and made them available for purchase by white settlers journeying west, impoverishing whole communities of Mexicans in the process.[4]

The Public Land Commission also presided over the land rights of Indigenous populations in California. After meeting with 402 tribal leaders, Indigenous landowners agreed to a series of eighteen treaties that relinquished their land claims to the US government. In return, Indigenous communities "had the right to use and occupy certain areas specifically described, and were promised supplies, tools, livestock, clothing, the services of agents, teachers, and carpenters, together with necessary buildings."[5] But as the gold rush was in full effect, white settlers were angry that Indigenous people had been promised the use of good land, and Congress rejected all eighteen treaties.[6] The lands that Indigenous groups relinquished thus also became public lands, relegating whole communities to reservations. In these two ways, the US government stripped Indigenous and Mexican Californio landowners of their property, claiming it as part of the public domain.

This immense acquisition of public lands is directly related to the construction of the transcontinental railroad. It was the first time that Congress had subsidized a railroad building project, and the government offered land grants on public land to fund railroad construction. The actual surveying of land began in the 1840s and 1850s, as "eastern and western cities proposed routes and promoted transcontinental railway bills in Congress."[7] In February of 1855, secretary of war and future Confederate president Jefferson Davis presented a report to Congress with "five possible railroad routes" to California from the Missouri River. Amid the tensions that would result in the Civil War, historian T. W. Van Metre explains, "In the popular mind the proposed Pacific railroad was a military necessity and one required to hold the nation together." Several years later, the war became a catalyst for the government's financial involvement in the project:

> One event in American railroad history, which grew directly out of the [Civil War] was the beginning of the first railroad to the Pacific Ocean.... In 1862 Congress chartered the Union Pacific Railroad to build a line westward from Omaha, Nebraska.
> At the same time the Central Pacific Railroad Company, a California corporation, was authorized to build a road eastward from Sacramento, to meet the Union Pacific. Both companies received huge grants of public land and substantial loans of money from Congress. This was the first instance of the direct subsidization of railroad construction by the federal government.[8]

Congress approved and largely funded this construction by passing the Pacific Railway Act in 1862 "to aid the construction of a railroad and telegraph line from the Missouri River to the Pacific Ocean, and to secure to the Government the use of the same for postal, military and other purposes."[9] Enabling federal funding in the form of land grants and bonds, the bill's beneficiaries were the Union Pacific Railroad Company, which built from Nebraska to the "western boundary of Nevada," and the Central Pacific Railroad Company, which built from San Francisco to the "eastern boundary of California."[10] In 1869, the Union Pacific and Central Pacific railroads connecting California to the East were complete, "the building of this long-hoped-for, long-planned railroad and of the railroads that followed . . . made possible by federal aid in the form of subsidy to railroad companies in lands and bonds."[11]

Along with two hundred feet of "right-of-way" land on both sides of the tracks (four hundred feet total), the government granted land for "stations, buildings, shops, depots, switches, sidetracks and turntables." Companies were also permitted to use the natural resources in the area, such as timber and stone, as building materials. When the Southern Pacific Railroad launched a line running from the Pacific Ocean to New Orleans—a move that deeply impacted what had recently become borderlands communities—these federal land grants remained essential. By 1875, the government had given railroad companies the right of way through public lands, meaning they were authorized to build anywhere the US considered public domain. Not only did this include lands previously seized from Indigenous and Mexican Californio property holders, but according to historian William Wilcox Robinson, the US government also "agreed to extinguish Indian titles where they conflicted with railroad titles."[12] In addition, each grant-awarded company received "odd-numbered alternate sections of land to the amount of twenty sections per mile." But as Robinson explains, "Since each regular government section contained 640 acres, the acreage granted per mile was, in theory, 12,800 acres."[13] Thus, in California alone, railroad companies "received title to 11,585,534.28 acres of California land, or about 11.4 percent of the state's area."[14] These companies were permitted to sell any land they did not end up using, which they did at $1.25 an acre (about $45 per acre today)—and kept the profits.[15]

The advent of the transcontinental railroad exemplifies the nation's commitment to westward expansion, industrial capitalism, and white supremacy. Stealing Indigenous and Mexican lands and reclassifying them as "public," the US government was complicit with railroad companies in building a hugely lucrative industry—one unfettered by regulations and propped up by congressional subsidies in the form of land grants and bonds. Structural violence was baked into the project, as the nonwhite populations inhabiting the region were left impoverished and exploited. Mexican American writers documented this violence, their work functioning not only as testimonies to these abuses but also as warnings to their communities. It is to these protest novels that we now turn.

The Squatter and the Don: A Bad Investment or Industry Cruelty?

María Amparo Ruiz de Burton wrote of these events in her 1885 novel *The Squatter and the Don*. She tells the story of Don Mariano Almar, patriarch of the Almar family, *hacendado* Californios in San Diego at risk of losing all they have due to Anglo squatters taking their land and killing their cattle.[16] In an attempt to avoid financial ruin, Don Mariano decides to invest in the construction of the Texas Pacific Railroad stretching from El Paso to San Diego. Unfortunately, this proves to be a disastrous financial move for Don Mariano and his associates, Mr. Mechlin and Mr. Holman, when an agreement between railroad magnates reroutes the line.

Don Mariano's financial demise reflects historical events steeped in the violence that railroad companies inflicted on San Diego's borderlands communities. While the federal government provided land grants and legislation to support railroad construction, companies like Southern Pacific also solicited money from local investors. In particular, a group of industry tycoons known as the Big Four engaged in this practice. Consisting of Leland Stanford (who would become governor of California), Collis Potter Huntington, Mark Hopkins, and Charles Crocker, the Big Four owned

Central Pacific Railroad in Northern California, and eventually Southern Pacific as well. As Evelyne Payen-Variéras argues, the group took advantage of regional competition to garner funds for their railroad projects, including by accepting private investments. She writes, "According to a list of Central Pacific stockholders compiled by the company for the US Secretary of the Treasury in June 1863, 229 stockholders out of 253 were residents of Sacramento County, 21 came from rural counties in California and only two appeared as residents of San Francisco."[17] Locals bought these shares to invest in the railroad because they believed its construction would bring booming business, tourism, and increased trade. Indeed, this is Don Mariano's mindset in *The Squatter and the Don*, as Californians throughout the state invested in railroads in the hopes of fostering local economic growth and obtaining financial stability for their families and communities. And railroad companies were all too happy to take their money.[18]

In Ruiz de Burton's narrative, Don Mariano invests in the Texas Pacific Railroad, which is building a new line from Marshall, Texas, to San Diego, where the novel takes place. Historically, Congress passed a bill on March 3, 1871, granting the company a charter for this construction. When Southern Pacific learned about the project, the Big Four saw it as a threat to their railroad line, and Huntington slowly started buying portions of the Galveston, Harrisburg, and San Antonio railroad that was under construction. By 1880, Huntington owned so much of it that he "[consolidated it] into a system," and Southern Pacific completed the line connecting San Antonio and El Paso.[19] Amid legal battles between the companies, Huntington struck a deal with Jay Gould, the owner of Texas Pacific, in 1881. Known as the Gould-Huntington Agreement, the companies determined:

> Under terms of this agreement the Texas and Pacific was to build no further than Sierra Blanca, ninety-two miles east of El Paso. The two systems would use the line to El Paso jointly, forming one continuous line to the coast. The Texas and Pacific relinquished its property rights and franchises west of El

Paso to the Southern Pacific. The agreement also provided for pooling, harmonious operation, and for the cooperation in the building of new lines.[20]

Thus, the Texas Pacific Railroad would no longer extend to San Diego, leaving local investors in dire financial straits. What's more, they and the whole region would suffer the economic loss of businesses the railroad would have brought in. As *The Squatter and the Don* makes clear, decisions made by the rich and powerful for personal gain subjected San Diegans to a fate of impoverishment. Ruiz de Burton exposes this systemic violence in her narrative condemning railroad barons' devotion to industrial capitalism at the expense of communities along the US-Mexico borderlands.

Although Don Mariano is a fictional character, Ruiz de Burton includes historical figures, such as former governor of California Leland Stanford, in the events in *The Squatter and the Don* to exhibit the real stakes in her story. She depicts Don Mariano and his associates, Mechlin and Holman, meeting with Stanford, one of the Big Four. The trio visits Stanford's office to implore him and his colleague Huntington to reconsider allowing Texas Pacific to build their railroad to San Diego. Stanford's response demonstrates the Big Four's disregard and scorn toward the borderlands communities they harmed in their quest to monopolize California's railroad industry. First, he justifies the magnates' actions by belittling San Diego's landscape, calling it a "most arid luckless region, where it never rains." Don Mariano counters, "That is the talk of San Francisco people," alluding to well-known regional rivalries, as the diverse regions of California were in competition for railroads to be constructed through their communities.[21] This exchange demonstrates a harmful laissez-faire philosophy; railroad companies were permitted to control how, where, and when to build railroads without any government oversight to ensure community welfare, even as federal land grants helped facilitate this massive endeavor. Holman replies in agricultural terms, explaining that fruit grows very well in Southern California and so offers a better crop yield than other regions during dry years. However, this agricultural argument is not enough to convince Stanford of San Diego's economic allure.

Switching tactics, the trio tries using pathos to appeal to Stanford. They explain that they have invested all of their money into the construction of the Texas Pacific Railroad. Their livelihoods depend on reaping the railroad's economic rewards; they will be ruined if the project does not go through. Dismissively, Stanford replies that they have plenty of cattle to subsist on, but Don Mariano explains that squatters have killed his cattle and, along with a storm that left most of his animals dead, he has very little remaining livestock: "I have only my land to rely upon for a living—nothing else. Hence my great anxiety to have the Texas Pacific. My land will be very valuable if we have a railroad and our county becomes more settled; but if not, my land, like everybody else's land in our county, will be unsaleable, worthless. A railroad is our only salvation."[22] This plea reveals an unfortunate irony, as the precarious circumstances created by industrial capitalists like Huntington and Stanford—the railroad itself—can be either the undoing or the salvation of Don Mariano and other local landowners.

Stanford remains unmoved by this emotional appeal and, making his priorities clear, retorts that he is a businessman. The three San Diegans reproachfully remind Stanford that since the government is subsidizing railroad construction, he and his business partners are accountable to Congress. Indignant, Stanford responds, "You don't seem to think of business principles. You forget that in business every one is for himself. . . . The American people mind their business, and know better than to interfere with ours."[23] Admitting that he and other railroad tycoons are in cahoots with the US government, Stanford is unapologetic about their shared objective to turn a profit by connecting the East and West Coasts. Even though San Diego's population would shrink by half as a result of Southern Pacific's interference, to Stanford it is simply the cost of doing business.[24]

In a last-ditch effort to compel Stanford to reassess his

position, Holman lectures him on the dangers of monopolies, adding that there is such a thing as a moral approach to business. He declares, "Monopolies should not exist when they become so powerful that they defy the law, and use their power to the injury of others." Stanford, rather coldly, puts the final nail in the coffin of the San Diegan trio's investment, replying, "Corporations have no souls, gentlemen, and I am no Carlylean hero-philanthropist. I am only a most humble *'public carrier.'* I do not aspire to anything more than taking care of my business.... If I don't cause distress some one else will. Distress there must be, bound to be in this world, in spite of all that your philanthropists might do or say to prevent it."[25] When the three men ask if it is worth the suffering it will inflict upon a whole community, Stanford only repeats this argument, seemingly with a clear conscience.

Stanford's dismissiveness and contempt throughout the meeting reflects the industrial capitalist philosophy of the late nineteenth century: turn a profit by any means necessary. Corruption and exploitation were par for the course, especially among railroad tycoons, their unscrupulous business practices even earning them the moniker *robber baron*. Stanford conveys as much by pointing out that there will always be someone causing distress to others for their own financial gain. This drive for profit and power led the railroad industry, with the help of the US government, to create inherently violent conditions that disenfranchised already marginalized people.

Ruiz de Burton concludes her novel with a chapter titled "Out With the Invader." It is here at the very end that she pulls back the curtain to reveal that her story is not strictly one of fiction but also reality. Essentially breaking the fourth wall, she speaks directly to her readers in this chapter, calling for an uprising against railroad companies. Noting their refusal to pay taxes, Ruiz de Burton denounces their behavior as an "excess of lawlessness."[26] Indeed, this allegation particularly applied to Southern Pacific, as the company refused to pay taxes in 1885 in response to what the magnates argued was unfair property taxation on the part of various California counties. The Big Four took the case all the way to the Supreme Court—and won.[27] The impunity these millionaires enjoyed, especially while so many Californians were suffering, infuriated Ruiz de Burton. She goes on to cite several letters written by Huntington to Southern Pacific lobbyist David D. Colton that were released to the public as a result of a different lawsuit—one filed by Colton's widow after she received what she considered little money from her husband's stock in the company. In one of the letters, dated March 7, 1877, Huntington writes explicitly about the influence he and his colleagues had over Congress: "I stayed in Washington two days to fix up a Railroad Committee in the Senate. *The Committee is just as we want it*, which is a very important thing for us."[28] Disclosing that the railroad lobby is able to persuade Congress to form favorable committees, Huntington offers a very clear admission of corruption and collusion in which federal legislation prioritizes railroad companies and their profits rather than the American people. It was such legislation that authorized squatters to take the fictional Don Mariano and his family's land and corporations to leave them destitute. Including Huntington's letter demonstrates that the novel is rooted in historical facts and thus strengthens Ruiz de Burton's call to action.

However, it is important to point out that her motivation for exposing this violence may not have necessarily been rooted in concern for all who inhabit the US-Mexico borderlands. In his article "The Whiteness of the Blush: The Cultural Politics of Racial Formation in the *Squatter and the Don*," John M. González complicates Ruiz de Burton's perspective, arguing that her anger and distress are also racially motivated. Her protagonist Don Mariano represents a class of formerly wealthy hacendado Californios—of which Ruiz de Burton was a member—whose proximity to whiteness shielded them from racist policies affecting nonwhite communities. That land was taken from "white" Californios—aristocrats in the former Mexican territory—is significant, their whiteness informing her argument for protecting their land and wealth. The railroad industry's growing political power jeopardized the Mexican racial hierarchy that safeguarded this class of people now residing in the United States. As González explains:

> In short, the railroad monopoly functions as an *imperium in imperio* that threatens to replace the nation's white citizenship with the corporate empire's white slavery. Delinking class difference from racial difference, corporations transform white Californios into Indians, white workers into the structural equivalent of black or Chinese workers, and US citizens into colonial subjects.[29]

Thus, although Ruiz de Burton does illuminate systemic violence enacted against a real community, her position remains problematic.

Yet Ruiz de Burton's fear of the consequences of this racial disruption was not unfounded, as racist legislation was a reality. Legislation targeting racialized groups was abundant and extremely alarming. With the 1855 Greaser Act, for example, the state "leased" Indigenous people and poor mestizos who were perceived as vagrants to work for large companies, essentially providing them with free labor. As Kayley Berger explains, "Since California was admitted as a 'free' state, the state lacked slave labor and so created these vagrancy statutes to meet their labor demands."[30] Industrialization and modernization were the state's priorities; exploiting disenfranchised groups of people, be they Indigenous or white-lusting Californios who lost their social status, was inconsequential. In what González calls the "corporate age of US empire," collaborations between legislative state bodies and powerful corporations created conditions that were inherently violent for nonwhite communities, justified in the name of business and profit.[31] With *The Squatter and the Don*, Ruiz de Burton exposes important facets of this violence along the nineteenth-century US-Mexico borderlands.

The Abuse of Mexican Immigrants in *Don Chipote*

Likewise, I argue that Daniel Venegas's 1928 novel *Las aventuras de Don Chipote; o, Cuando los pericos mamen* (*The Adventures of Don Chipote; or, When Parrots Breast-Feed*) is also a protest novel that illuminates the ongoing state and corporate violence afflicting nonwhite borderlands communities. The book, set in the 1920s, features the story of Don Chipote, a Mexican immigrant who leaves home after a friend convinces him that he will become wealthy in the United States. Don Chipote finds work on *el traque*—that is, laying down railroad tracks—as railroad companies continue to expand well into the first decades of the twentieth century. Revealing the harsh exploitation of immigrant labor along the US-Mexico borderlands, Venegas offers, in scholar Nicolás Kanellos's words, a "socio-historic testimony on the labor conditions, culture, and expressive forms of the *braceros* at that time."[32]

Although laborers of Irish and Chinese descent are generally more prominent in the historical imagination of US railroad construction, Jeffrey Marcos Garcílazo shows that Mexican immigrants comprised over two-thirds of the railroad workforce between 1880 and 1930.[33] In particular, these Mexican laborers, known as *traqueros*, "far outnumbered all other groups of immigrant and or native-born labor on the tracks in the Southwest."[34] This was in part due to the feverish anti-Chinese racism running rampant in the late nineteenth century and, most impactfully, the Chinese Exclusion Act of 1882. By the 1890s, Southern Pacific had begun replacing their Chinese workforce with Mexican immigrants. More significantly, the Mexican Revolution from 1910 to 1920 led many to flee the violence and poverty created by the bloody internal conflict, increasing the numbers of Mexican immigrant laborers on US soil. Finally, the National Origins Act of 1924 established quotas that restricted immigration from places like Asia and Eastern Europe. Yet as Rachel Conrad Bracken explains, "Notably, these restrictions did not apply to nations in the Western Hemisphere, so that southwestern growers and railroad companies would still have access to cheap

Mexican migrant labor."[35] Thus, immigrants like Don Chipote were in the majority on el traque.

Just as Ruiz de Burton addresses her audience in her call to action, Venegas speaks directly to his readers in *Don Chipote*. However, rather than writing an epilogue like Ruiz de Burton, Venegas breaks his story's narrative flow to periodically interject his perspective throughout the book. In a move Kanellos calls "historiciz[ing] his narrative and document[ing] social reality," Venegas reveals early on that in fact he used to be a worker on el traque. This decision to insert his own lived experience while narrating the story of the fictional Don Chipote communicates the authenticity of the issues he presents in the novel. Thus, details of abuse are not mere authorial machinations but a "protest not only of the mistreatment of Chicanos but the complicity of the governments of Mexico and the United States in their exploitation." Venegas meant for his work to function as a warning, originally publishing *Don Chipote* in Spanish to caution other Chicanos about the violence they would face if they migrated to the United States for work.[36]

The novel features many instances of this violence, demonstrating the utter exploitation and mistreatment of Mexican migrants. One of the early incidents is Don Chipote's arrival at the border, when an officer "[takes] note of Don Chipote's grimy appearance" and directs him to a communal shower where other men are undressing.[37] The degradation and shock of this moment are clear, especially since the language barrier prevented Don Chipote from understanding where he was being sent. As the other men explain, all Mexican migrants must undergo this bathing ritual "to comply with the procedure that the American government had created expressly for all Mexicans crossing into their land."[38] Indeed, the practice was mandated by a public health ordinance put in place in the 1910s as more Mexicans were journeying north during the Mexican Revolution. In conjunction with this treatment, the US government assured corporate associates that there would be enough Mexican immigrants coming into the country to provide a cheap labor force for the railroad and agricultural industries.

Despite the mortification and vulnerability of the situation, Don Chipote very willingly undresses, thinking, "If this was the only thing he had to do, it was not worth fussing over." But Venegas as the narrator disapproves of his protagonist's decision, criticizing him for "actually taking pleasure in the first humiliation that the *gringo* forces on Mexican immigrants."[39] Don Chipote's clothes are also taken to be "placed in a fumigating steam"—a practice that, as Conrad Bracken explains, fumigated immigrants' clothing in chemicals that contained "the pesticide Zyklon B [which] was later used in Nazi gas chambers."[40] This harmful fumigation and the communal baths were so humiliating and dehumanizing that some immigrants pushed back, namely in the El Paso Bath Riots of 1917, in which border officers took photographs of nude immigrant women.[41] With Don Chipote, Venegas adds insult to injury; when his clothes are returned to him, they have shrunk and now he is the "laughingstock of all those who saw him."[42]

Venegas's running commentary throughout the novel—what Kanellos calls historicizing the narrative—thus reflects Mexican immigrants' very real experiences upon entering the United States, including those of the author himself. In addition to the degrading baths and dangerous mode of disinfecting their clothing, Mexican immigrants' arms were sometimes marked with the word *admitted* in permanent ink after their inspections. Alexandra Minna Stern writes that Mexicans crossing at the Laredo, Texas, border regularly grew angry about this labeling practice, which was implemented in 1916 on the US Public Health Service's (USPHS) orders. After the Mexican consul demanded that the USPHS cease this practice of stamping "indelible ink" on Mexican migrants, the Mexican secretariat of foreign affairs got involved. In response, the US Immigration Service defended the stamping practice as more convenient than "highly impractical identification cards and suggested that it effectively shielded Mexicans from the harassment of Texas Rangers." Articulating the importance of this incident, Stern argues, "This confrontation illustrates the centrality of medicalization to the solidification of the border.... In tandem, these two trends—medicalization and militarization—worked to create a regime of eugenic gatekeeping on the US-Mexican border that aimed to ensure the putative purity of the 'American' family-nation while generating long-lasting stereotypes of Mexicans as filthy, lousy, and prone to irresponsible breeding."[43] Justifying this treatment with claims about science and public health was crucial in state efforts to limit border access. These efforts would soon become more militarized when the Border Patrol was established in 1924—a militaristic endeavor that would only increase throughout the twentieth century.

Venegas's interjections as narrator in *Don Chipote* do more than reference true encounters and events. He offers his own opinions without pretense of objectivity—criticizing Don Chipote's acquiescence to the bathing procedure, for example—and thereby prompts a sense of outrage among his readers, who are intended to be fellow Mexican laborers. It is a mode of literary activism, one in which the narrator's role is as important as the protagonist's. As Paul Fallon contends, "By shifting the referent, the text interrupts the scene, reminds readers of their own activity in generating the fiction, then more intimately invites the reader to compare his/her experience with the protagonist's."[44] Welcoming the reader to participate in the story—inviting action from those expected to be passive—effectively conveys a message of denunciation and resistance, and brings about a borderlands consciousness.

Venegas maintains this tactic throughout the novel, speaking directly to the audience when Don Chipote boards the train that will take him to his new job on el traque: "Now, readers, here you have Don Chipote on his way to California. Will he make it? Those of you who have been hooked into working on the *traque*, tell me. Does he have much left to go?"[45] This interruption grabs readers' attention and indeed explicitly requests a response rooted in their own experiences. Having secured this attention, Venegas goes on to condemn US hypocrisy; a nation supposedly committed to democracy and religiosity that does "not hesitate to kick Mexicans around."[46] This narrative interruption not only enables Venegas to air his grievances against the *gringo*, but also provides an opportunity for readers to consider and attest to the ways they have been treated. In doing so, Venegas encourages his audience to be active participants in protest rather than passive consumers of a book.

After denouncing how Mexicans are treated in the United States, Venegas returns to the story and introduces Papá Suplai / Papa Supply; that is, the railroad company supply store that sells food and goods to the laborers.[47] The name is sarcastic, highlighting the condescending paternalism of these corporate depots. Since el traque was generally located in isolated areas far from towns, buying necessary items from the company's store was laborers' only option, and many companies took advantage of the opportunity to raise prices. These stores also often took payment directly out of workers' paychecks, sometimes leaving them indebted to the company store for simply buying food. This created an exploitative cycle in which the laborer was willing to endure any kind of abuse on the job: they were in debt to the company, and thus had to continue working in a terrible work environment. Venegas as narrator describes this experience with Papa Supply:

> There is only one day they get excited and that's payday. . . . But this enthusiasm at receiving their paychecks usually ends up in rage, because, obligated to purchase their fortnight's provisions from the Supply, he who is granted the authority by the railroad company takes out whatever he wants from each of their paychecks; and the result are poor workers, for all they try to economize, always come away with the short end of the stick.[48]

Thus, in addition to raising prices to take advantage of workers, the railroad company authorized whoever was in charge of the supply store "to take out whatever he wants from their paychecks." As Venegas warns throughout the novel, this unfettered treatment of laborers was the norm on el traque.

He has no shortage of examples that expose the harsh conditions and abuse of railroad laborers. One incident involves Don

Chipote's dog, Sufrelambre, who drinks from the workers' water barrel. The angry foreman sends Don Chipote back to the depot, more than a mile away, to get another barrel, which he must carry on his back. Here, the narrator intervenes with a story from his own life about the mistreatment he has suffered while laying railroad tracks. Venegas tells of the time a foreman, seemingly on a whim, demanded that he and his fellow traqueros replace a "'sweech,' or direction changer" thirty minutes before a train was due to pass through, making it an incredibly dangerous assignment. When they completed the task, the foreman yelled at them "in a manner so vile that unable to take any more of his insults, I talked back to him." In response, the foreman struck Venegas and Venegas hit him back. He was then fired from the railroad company and was not paid for any of the time he worked there. Venegas explains that such incidents are daily occurrences and clarifies that this is the type of foreman who punishes Don Chipote in this particular story.[49] By historicizing the narrative with a seemingly comical situation—that is, a poor dog owner pays for his dog's sin—Venegas shocks the audience, revealing what is actually real treatment of real people.

The exploitation of Mexican immigrant workers on el traque was heavily rooted in racism and white supremacy. Their willingness to work under difficult conditions made them a valuable labor force, but many white foremen took advantage of that and subjected them to danger and abuse. Garcílazo found that this dehumanization of Mexican immigrant workers was rampant. He discusses an Arizona newspaper that characterized the life of a Mexican as equivalent to that of a "mongrel dog." The article went on to say that foremen "speculated that the term 'greaser' originated from the way insults 'slide off Mexicans like water off a duck's back.'"[50] Likewise, *Santa Fe Magazine*—an Atchison, Topeka, and Santa Fe Railroad Company publication—printed a story in which a white foreman insists that "a child's mind matures and the Mexican never does."[51] The article consequently advocated for treating Mexican immigrant laborers like children—with underdeveloped brains. All of these documented abuses reflect Venegas's portrayal in *Las aventuras de*

Don Chipote. His efforts to historicize his narrative and share this information with a Mexican audience as a cautionary tale were successful indeed, as he ultimately published the novel in Mexico City.

Conclusion

To offer some closing thoughts about the nature of protest in *The Squatter and the Don* and *Las aventuras de Don Chipote,* I want to note the authors' different pathways to publication. Ruiz de Burton wrote under the pseudonym C. Loyal, so that publishers would assume that a man—probably a white man, by the surname—had authored *The Squatter and the Don*. Daniel Venegas initially printed *Las aventuras de Don Chipote* in the Los Angeles Spanish-language newspaper *El herald de México* in 1928 and was eventually able to publish it as a book in Mexico. In 2000, Arte Público Press at the University of Houston recovered and republished Venegas's novel, over seventy-two years after its original distribution. That these two authors managed to publish their work at all is remarkable. Despite the difficulties that the Mexican American community has faced in voicing their resistance to exploitation and abuse, they were able to historicize their narratives and get their stories out into the world.

It is quite telling that the historical record confers the title of "Orange County's first convicted felon" to a twenty-two-year-old Mexican American woman who hung her clothes to dry over some railroad tracks as an act of protest. *The Squatter and the Don* and *Las aventuras de Don Chipote* underscore such mistreatment, their fictional accounts reflecting countless real experiences of abuse. Ruiz de Burton and Venegas weave their borderland consciousness into their narratives, directly addressing their readership to denounce railroad companies and the US government, disrupt the imagined community of the nation, and call the people of the US-Mexico borderlands to action. Their novels expose the violence inflicted upon Mexican American and other nonwhite communities through US nation-building efforts in the nineteenth and early twentieth centuries, as the government engaged in widespread land theft, was complicit with the railroad industry, and justified racism, exploitation, and poverty in service to capitalism and Manifest Destiny. Indeed, they demonstrate that violence was part and parcel of these nation-building projects, rooted in a staunch dedication to westward expansion, white supremacy, and reinforcing wealthy, white, male citizenry. As literary activism of the US-Mexico borderlands, these authors challenge their own exclusion in the imagined community of the United States.

CHAPTER THREE

"MAY WE BREAK THE SPELL OF THE OFFICIAL STORY"

The Criminalization of Refugees of Color Represented in Demetria Martínez's *Mother Tongue* (1994) and *Confessions of a Berlitz-Tape Chicana* (2005)

One evening a few years ago, I received a call for clothing donations for a Central American woman whose child was hospitalized. She had just arrived in the United States and the clothing she came with would not keep her warm in our New Mexican winter. I spent the evening at Walmart buying winter clothing for the woman and brought it to her the next day. I found out that the child was transported to the hospital by US Customs and Border Protection (CBP). I felt the conviction to visit with the woman and her child to offer any help, and when I arrived there were two CBP agents standing outside the patient's door. I spent a few hours with the child and mother, and she told me the story of their escape from Central America. Due to gang violence, she and her partner—the patient's father—decided to travel north with their child. Her partner had been detained by CBP while the woman and child came to the hospital. Later that day while I was visiting, the woman found out that her partner had been transferred to a jail in a small town in southern New Mexico. We figured out a way to send money to his commissary account so he could make phone calls from the jail to the hospital room the child was staying in to check on his partner and hospitalized child. All the while, the CBP agents stood outside.

Eventually, the agents requested to speak with the woman, and she asked me if I could join as an interpreter. I agreed and we met in a conference room outside the pediatric unit. The CBP agents wanted her to sign a form indicating that she would appear before an immigration judge regarding her asylum claim. They assured her that they would leave once she signed. When she demanded to know what would happen to her partner, they simply shrugged their shoulders and stated that he was in jail and would have his own day in court. The arbitrary nature of this treatment and the apathy of the CBP agents hit me like a brick. The woman signed the paperwork with tears in her eyes, and shared with me later that she had conflicting feelings about being permitted to stay in the United States to make a case for her asylum claim while her partner, the father of her child, was detained in a jail cell with no command of English and very little money to make the calls necessary to prepare his own claim. The CBP agents took the document and left.

The next week, the child was well enough to be discharged and by then I had arranged for my local church to provide money, food, and support for the mother. We were able to get her a prepaid cell phone, which allowed her to have regular contact with her partner and to get in touch with a relative on the East Coast. Their original plan was to stay with this relative, and so she made the difficult decision to head east with her child, but without her partner. The last I heard of her, she had found a job cleaning homes while living with her relative, but I did not learn the fate of her partner or the outcome of her asylum claim. I think of her often.

She was on my heart as I researched and prepared this chapter in which I discuss the sanctuary movement of the 1980s when, in the wake of civil wars in Guatemala and El Salvador, people fleeing the two countries sought refuge for themselves and their children in the United States. Activists, aid workers, and multidenominational church networks provided food, shelter, and support for these refugees, building the sanctuary movement despite the risk and reality of severe repercussions. They participated in resistance to systemic violence propagated by the United States. Moreover, many of the truly horrific circumstances that obliged Guatemalans (the majority of whom were Indigenous) and Salvadorans to leave their home countries were caused by US policy, law, and political meddling. Yet in the 1980s, the United States punished these refugees for heeding their survival instincts—the very human compulsion to seek safety—and also punished those American citizens and legal residents who dared to resist inhumane laws to help them.

This chapter centers the work of Demetria Martínez, a Chicana poet and journalist who aided two pregnant Salvadoran women at the US-Mexico border in 1986. The following year, Martínez was indicted on federal charges of conspiracy and went to federal court. She was ultimately found not guilty on First Amendment grounds, but many other participants in the sanctuary movement were convicted and faced jail time or probation. Martínez subsequently wrote about her experience, first as fiction in her novel *Mother Tongue* (1996) and later in her memoir, *Confessions of a Berlitz-Tape Chicana* (2005). These texts offer a point of departure to analyze Martínez's work in the sanctuary movement of the 1980s and US asylum and sanctuary laws more broadly. I argue that nation-states such as the United States create and utilize a language of criminalization to justify denying refugees entry into the country as well as to racialize and persecute those who are already there. Writing like Martínez's illuminates this racialization and criminalization, and works to restore the collective memory of those silenced by the dominant narrative criminalizing them. As such, she and other participants in the sanctuary movement of the 1980s created a memory community and alternate narrative that exposes the state violence inflicted on refugees of color.

Language of Criminalization: *Refugee* versus *Asylum Seeker*

Terminology regarding persons fleeing their home country to seek refuge elsewhere is often loaded, the language parsed and divided in arbitrary ways that obscure true suffering. Elie Wiesel, a survivor of the Holocaust, acknowledged these distinctions in a 1985 speech at the Inter-American Symposium on Sanctuary in Tucson, Arizona, right in the middle of the sanctuary movement. Addressing the crowd, he asked, "What has been done to the word *refuge*? In the beginning the word sounded beautiful. A *refuge* meant 'home.' It welcomed you, protected you, gave you warmth and hospitality. Then we added one single phoneme, one letter, *e*, and the sensitive term *refuge* became *refugee*, connoting something negative."[1] A refugee himself, Wiesel's analysis recognizes how this terminology is corrupted by the language of criminalization, transforming a compassionate welcome into suspicion and hostility that mask the very humanity of those seeking safe haven.

Likewise, the US government's terminology regarding immigration classifications creates significant distinctions that inform understandings of legitimacy and illegitimacy. This is particularly pertinent in the legal differentiation between *refugee* and *asylum seeker*. The US Immigration and Nationality Act (INA) defines a *refugee* as "any person who is outside any country of such person's nationality or, in the case of a person having no nationality, is outside any country in which such person last habitually resided, and who is unable or unwilling to return to, and is unable or unwilling to avail himself or herself of the protection of, that country because of persecution or a well-founded fear of persecution on account of race, religion, nationality, membership in a particular social group, or political opinion."[2] While this initial definition seems appropriately broad enough to be inclusive of all individuals that fit the above description, in practice the numerical ceiling for admission of refugees effectively limits it. This refugee admissions ceiling is determined by the president of the United States and goes through congressional approval every year. Along with the refugee admissions ceiling, Section 207 of the INA, titled "Annual admission of refugees and admission of emergency situation refugees," goes on to stipulate additional criteria for admission into the United States under refugee status. These criteria include a specific number of refugees the United States will accept every year, depending on country of origin—numbers that have fluctuated in recent years, particularly under the Trump administration. This section also explains that refugee status can be conferred with priority entry to the United States if recommended by the president or attorney general.[3]

In contrast, asylum seekers are a distinct legal category. Under the Refugee Act and subsequent regulations, to qualify for asylum an applicant must first meet the definition of a refugee. Notably, the law states, "Any alien who is physically present in the United States or who arrives in the United States (whether or not at a designated port of arrival and including an alien who is brought to the United States after having been interdicted in international or United States waters), irrespective of such alien's status, may apply for asylum."[4] Beyond the statutory requirement of meeting the refugee definition, there are distinct legal differences between asylum seekers and refugees. For example, the *Report to Congress on Proposed Refugee Admissions for Fiscal Year 2021* differentiates between a person with refugee status and a person with asylum status: "While asylum *applicants* are not eligible for the Reception & Placement assistance offered to refugees . . . those who have been granted asylum status under Section 208 of the INA are eligible for other assistance and services funded by the HHS Office of Refugee Resettlement (ORR)." The report continues:

> The United States anticipates receiving more than 300,000 new asylum claimants and refugees in Fiscal Year (FY) 2021. Pursuant to Section 207(d) of the Immigration and Nationality Act (INA), the President proposes resettling up to 15,000 refugees under the FY 2021 refugee admissions ceiling, and anticipates receiving new asylum claims that include more than 290,000 individuals. This proposed refugee admissions ceiling reflects the continuing backlog of over 1.1 million asylum-seekers who are awaiting adjudication of their claims inside the United States, and it accounts for the arrival of refugees whose resettlement in the United States was delayed due to the COVID-19 pandemic.[5]

While there is no admissions ceiling for asylum seekers, the backlog of pending cases as well as a political climate that is hostile toward asylum seekers effectively denies them their legal right to seek asylum in the United States.

Emphasizing the distinction between refugees and asylum seekers, this 2021 report aligns with the definitions outlined in the 1951 Convention and Protocol Related to the Status of Refugees. A 2010 introductory note to the 1951 protocol describes the parameters of asylum seeking laid out by the Convention:

> The Convention further stipulates that, subject to specific exceptions, refugees should not be penalized for their illegal entry or stay. This recognizes that the seeking of asylum can require refugees to breach immigration rules. Prohibited penalties might include being charged with immigration or criminal offences relating to the seeking of asylum, or being arbitrarily detained purely on the basis of seeking asylum. Importantly, the Convention contains various safeguards against the expulsion of refugees.[6]

Additionally, the 1948 Universal Declaration of Human Rights states, "(1) Everyone has the right to seek and to enjoy in other countries asylum from persecution; (2) This right may not be invoked in the case of prosecutions genuinely arising from non-political crimes or from acts contrary to the purposes and principles of the United Nations."[7] While the United States has signed on to both international conventions, it has clearly opted to overlook these provisos when dealing with Central American refugees fleeing violence in their home countries. Those who present themselves at the US-Mexico border are labeled asylum seekers, arrested, and held in detention centers or kept in limbo through programs like the Remain in Mexico policy—a very different experience with US bureaucracy than that encountered by people with refugee status. For asylum seekers, this rhetorical and legal distinction not only results in harsh treatment and dangerous conditions but also works to indict their very existence. I argue that language of criminalization within the US legal code regarding asylum seekers creates what Galtung calls latent violence, "something which is not there, yet might easily come about. . . . There is latent violence when the situation is so unstable that the actual realization level 'easily' decreases."[8] Latent violence permeates the US-Mexico border, as people seeking asylum from violence in their home countries are met with mistreatment and built-in bias, manifested in the very language used to identify them.

Criminalizing Central American Refugees in the 1980s

In the 1980s, amid growing conflicts in Central America, the US Department of Justice (DOJ) under the Reagan administration had a significant say in whether asylum seekers from countries like El Salvador and Guatemala would be granted asylum or refugee status.[9] The Refugee Act of 1980, signed by President Carter but enacted under Reagan, created new parameters that significantly curtailed the number of individuals to be granted asylum. Consequently, as table 1 shows, the number of refugee arrivals far outweighed the asylum grants conferred in the 1980s. By legally differentiating between refugees and asylum seekers, the US government essentially singled out as suspect those who fled their home country without prior permission from the United States, leading to their claims of persecution being viewed with hostility and largely denied.

The Refugee Act of 1980 provided the language of criminalization to legally justify such treatment, as the official distinction in this law between refugees and asylum seekers encourages state actors to harass, detain, and deport certain people fleeing persecution and protect others. In effect, it automatically places those who arrive unannounced and claim asylum at the US-Mexico border under suspicion of potentially lying about the violence they faced in their home countries and taking advantage of the "good will" of the United States. The term *asylum seeker* thus empowered CBP and INS (and now ICE) to enact violence against people characterized as such: to detain those who present themselves at the US-Mexico border, deny them access to filing asylum claims, and deport them. It criminalizes as well as racializes the categorization of "asylum seeker." Crucially, the majority of these refugees are Indigenous or

Table 1. Refugee Admission and Asylum Grants, 1980–1989, Bureau of Population, Refugees, and Migration, *Report to Congress on Proposed Refugee Admissions for Fiscal Year 2021*.

Fiscal Year	Refugee Arrivals	Individual Asylum Grants	Annual Totals
1980	207,116	1,104	208,220
1981	159,252	1,175	160,427
1982	98,096	3,909	102,005
1983	61,218	7,215	68,433
1984	70,393	8,278	78,671
1985	67,704	4,585	72,289
1986	62,146	3,359	65,505
1987	64,528	4,062	68,590
1988	76,483	5,531	82,014
1989	107,070	6,942	114,012

Black. Thus, the foundation of the legal guidelines dictating how refugees can enter the United States is a settler-colonial one. This follows a long history of weaving euphemisms into legislation in order to displace and put Indigenous and Black people in harm's way. One such example can be found in the Declaration of Independence in the use of the phrase "merciless Indian savages." This connotes a sense of innate, uncontrollable violence in Indigenous people, suggesting that whatever fate befalls them—including genocide and displacement—is their fault.[10] Likewise, settler colonialism is at the root of the legal definition of *asylum seeker*, as the mostly Black and Indigenous individuals given this label must overcome inherent suspicion and prove they are worthy of the aid they seek. As with the "Indian savage," this language implies that any brutality directed toward asylum seekers is warranted as well as justified by US law.

Within this context, the US government deliberately sought to deny asylum to Central American refugees and deport them under the Refugee Act of 1980. According to Karen Musalo, "Those who reached the US were subject to policies that had as their stated objective the 'detention and quick deportation' of asylum seekers. They were targeted with coercive tactics by the then Immigration and Naturalization Service (INS) while in detention, intended to pressure them to sign a form accepting 'voluntary departure,' thereby abandoning their right to seek asylum." Validated by the language of criminalization, this treatment is deemed acceptable even when proof of persecution exists in abundance. For example, Musalo found that

> INS practices as applied to Salvadorans were successfully challenged in *Orantes-Hernandez v. Meese*, with the court ordering a range of procedures to assure that Salvadorans were informed of, and able to avail themselves of the right to seek asylum. In issuing its ruling in *Orantes-Hernandez*, the court made extensive findings of fact, including that a "substantial number of Salvadorans who flee El Salvador possess a well-founded fear of persecution," and that the persecutors were "primarily Salvadoran military and security forces."[11]

Additionally, *American Baptist Churches v. Thornburgh*, a 1990 class action lawsuit brought by churches and organizations on behalf of over five hundred thousand Salvadoran and Guatemalan asylum applicants, presented violations of the "United States Constitution, International law, and the Refugee Act of 1980" made by Immigrations and Naturalization Service (INS) and the Executive Office for Immigration Review (EOIR).[12] In the lawsuit, the "plaintiffs alleged that INS and EOIR processed the application on the basis of improper foreign policy considerations, border enforcement considerations, and political and ideological beliefs, and not based on the legislative standards under the Refugee Act of 1980."[13] After five years of litigation, this case was ultimately settled.

The US government's political and militaristic meddling into Central American countries' conflicts gravely exacerbated the conditions of migrants seeking asylum in the United States. Significantly, Salvadoran and Guatemalan refugees in particular were fleeing conditions of violence due in part to US interference in the countries' respective civil wars. This political meddling is well documented; indeed, it was the United States that was arming the death squads that were on a killing rampage, all in the name of fighting communism. In El Salvador, the Revolutionary Government Junta staged a military coup d'etat in October of 1979, forcing sitting president Carlos Humberto Romero into exile so that the military could place its own leaders into power. By 1980, two more juntas (postrevolution governing bodies) had replaced these leaders. Leftist guerrillas opposed the military government and, along with other communist organizations, formed the Farabundo Martí National Liberation Front (FMLN). In support of the government's fight against communism, the Reagan administration provided over $1 billion in aid and weapons to the Salvadoran dictatorship in the 1980s. It is estimated that "75,000 [people were] killed, 7,000 disappeared, and 500,000 were displaced."[14] In response to this very violent period in El Salvador, with US political and military support, many people fled north to the United States to seek refuge.

There is a similar story of US meddling in the civil war in Guatemala. This war started in 1960 when leftist guerrillas began fighting against the US-backed Guatemalan autocratic government. In the 1970s, right-wing leaders installed paramilitary groups to persecute and kill those who were sympathetic to the guerrilla fighters or communism more broadly. Labor activists, for example, were also targets of violence. The Inter-American Human Rights Commission wrote a scathing report in October 1981 accusing the Guatemalan government of executing and disappearing thousands of people in the 1970s. According to the Commission for Historical Clarification, a board supported by the United Nations, 83 percent of the persons killed were Mayan, and 93 percent of human rights violations were committed by agents of the Guatemalan state and military.[15] As in El Salvador, the Reagan administration gave the Guatemalan government over $33 million in aid in the 1980s, also in support of fighting communism.

The United States' involvement in these violent conflicts

shows that the US bore responsibility for the masses of people who fled Guatemala and El Salvador in search of refuge. Yet rather than accepting this responsibility, the regulations put forth by the Reagan administration and the Refugee Act of 1980 characterized them as runaway communists and thus denied them refugee status and asylum. Moreover, the category of *asylum seeker* stigmatizes and criminalizes certain migrants, particularly those who arrive at the US-Mexico border, the majority of whom are people of color. The US government has used this category since the 1980s to construct an official narrative that justifies state violence. In doing so, it has also created a volatile context in which latent violence bubbles at the border and will explode in somatic violence when a person of color has the audacity to present themselves and claim asylum in order to survive.

Breaking the Spell: Demetria Martínez and the Protection of Collective Memory

This diaspora of Central Americans into the United States—and the official narrative that tries to negate that violence—has inspired important accounts of refugee experiences. The Central American community in the United States is easily erased, as the dominant culture lumps all Latinx groups together, and it does not help that the majority of Latinxs are Mexican, Puerto Rican, and Cuban. It is thus crucial to document the atrocities faced in Central America as well as the injustices and violence inflicted by INS in the United States. This is what Demetria Martínez has done with her novel *Mother Tongue* (1996) and memoir *Confessions of a Berlitz-Tape Chicana* (2005). Significantly, Martínez is not a refugee herself but was a sanctuary activist, drawing on her interactions with refugees and other activists, and writing through the lens of a Chicana poet and journalist. Refusing to let Central American refugee experiences be erased or forgotten, she and others have constructed what Kelli

Lyon-Johnson calls a "memory community." Writing about Latina novelists and the Salvadoran civil war, Lyon-Johnson argues:

> Collective memory is contingent on the politics of who and what is remembered, who does the remembering, and how those memories are used in the name of national, ethnic, and cultural identity. Dead bodies also have political uses. The Salvadoran government exploited, tortured, murdered, and disappeared Salvadoran bodies during the Civil War, agents of Salvadoran collective memory. Benítez, Limón, and Martínez retrieve and reanimate Salvadoran bodies through narrative acts of memory. In doing so, they create a memory community in the United States across national, linguistic, and cultural boundaries.[16]

Through her work, Martínez actively contributes to the memory community of ravaged populations that have been violently discarded, both by their own governments and the United States. It is this memory community that brings about a borderlands consciousness, as those seeking refuge refuse to forget the violence they witnessed and endured in their home countries and denounce the injustice of being refused entry to a country that not only grants asylum but also has enabled the violence they fled.

Martínez is explicit in her intention to salvage these stories and to challenge the official narrative espoused by the US and Central American governments about what happened in the 1980s. In the introduction to *Confessions*, she explains:

> I'm no writer of manifestos; I'm a storyteller. As such, my job is to aid and abet, inspire and incite, refresh and console. I hope that you, the reader, will join me in an exchange.... We're in this plot together, no matter how different our backgrounds and beliefs. Our stories entwine like trumpet vines. Together may we break the spell of the official story and grant ourselves and the gods the open-ended destiny that is our right.[17]

Martínez invites the reader to "break the spell of the official story" propagated by the Reagan administration. In her writing, she exposes the real violence Salvadoran refugees faced in their home country, at the US-Mexico border, and living as undocumented persons in the United States fleeing INS. Breaking the spell of the official story pierces open a festering wound—one that, as Gloria Anzaldúa famously put it, is a grating of the third world against the first, and leads to a borderlands consciousness as well. The infection of erasure and violence seeps from the wound, but the healing begins with the documentation of atrocities, deportations, and deaths, and the creation of memory communities that can righteously demand justice.

Martínez's work offers various examples that combat the official story and break that spell. One way that she exposes the violence against Central American refugees is by writing about their racialization within migration processes, lore, and experiences. Her novel *Mother Tongue* features a Chicana sanctuary activist from New Mexico named María who provides aid to undocumented Salvadoran refugee José Luis, who is fleeing political persecution. The racialization of Central Americans is apparent almost immediately when María receives extensive instructions from the movement network detailing how to ensure that José Luis avoids attention from INS when she picks him up from the airport. A letter from her friend Soledad specifies that even his clothing must look a certain way: "The Border Patrol looks for 'un-American' clothing. I remember the time they even checked out a woman's blouse tag right there in the airport—'Hecho en El Salvador.' It took us another year and the grace of God to get her back up after she was deported." María also learns that she should tell José Luis to appear and behave as "Mexican" as possible, and to even memorize the names of Mexican cities in case he gets detained by INS. According to Soledad, "These are the kind of crazy things la migra asks about when they think they have a Central American."[18]

As these instructions demonstrate, the measures to which Central American refugees were subjected—even out of necessity by the sanctuary activists helping them—have roots in racialized violence against Indigenous communities. The problematics of "looking Mexican" as opposed to "looking Central American"—that presenting as Mexican is safer—reveal the settler-colonial violence and racism inherent in Mexican mestizaje, because looking too Indigenous is a threat to their safety but looking like a mestizo most likely is not. Racism against Indigenous communities is pervasive in Mexico as well as in the United States, making presenting as Indigenous in either of these countries a dangerous experience. According to Catherine Nolan-Ferell's oral history and archival research on the 1970s and 1980s, Mexican attitudes toward Guatemalan refugees tended to be discriminatory, particularly when Indigenous Guatemalans spoke native languages and wore traditional clothing. Nolan-Ferell discusses a Mexican school teacher who said that "'being Guatemalan was seen as something very bad for Mexicans,' and that using the word chapín (a nickname for Guatemalans) was considered a significant insult that could lead to fights."[19]

The discrimination Guatemalan refugees face while traveling through Mexico is well known, especially the derisive insult mentioned above. This disparagement and differentiation between Central Americans and Mexicans is clearly racial; the former is considered Indigenous and the latter mestizo. This not only exposes the racism baked into mestizaje identity in Mexican culture but also that racializing Central American refugees works to criminalize their indigeneity.

Martínez's work demonstrates how this racialization of asylum seekers leads to their criminalization. In the chapter "Driving while Brown" of *Confessions*, she recounts the experience of a friend, columnist Roberto Rodriguez, who was detained in a US Border Patrol (USBP) checkpoint forty-five minutes outside of Las Cruces, New Mexico, while driving on I-25. The officers gave him no reason for his detention, only that USBP has "broad discretion when it comes to questioning anybody 'about your immigration status and other suspicious circumstances.'"[20] Rodriguez filed a complaint. He subsequently received a letter from Alan Gordon, acting chief Border

Patrol agent of that sector, confirming that Rodriguez was guilty of "suspicious behavior." Gordon explained that Rodriguez was taking an indirect route from Los Angeles to Tucson to Albuquerque. Rodriguez was on a book tour in these cities to promote a recent publication. According to Gordon, he was also driving a rental car that was too clean: "Articles such as clothing, toiletries, or foodstuffs—items 'consistent with persons in travel'—were nowhere in sight. Rodriguez had his belongings in the trunk, along with stacks of books."[21] For a man with brown skin, having a clean car constitutes suspicious behavior.

Rodriguez's experience illustrates that USBP criminalizes people of color for simply existing. As he explained to Martínez, "This isn't even an issue of immigration. I was traveling to nonborder cities. I'm a US citizen."[22] But as a dark-skinned Latino, state agents were suspicious of his citizenship and location, and regarded Rodriguez as suspect on sight. Thus, it is not only refugees of color who face criminalization and state violence but also American citizens of color. The issue is not one of immigration but rather of social justice; for racialized people, racism is pervasive in everyday life.

Research on the legalities of racial profiling corroborates the experiences that Martínez documents in her work. In a 2019 article published in the *Cornell Law Review*, Pablo Chapablanco explains the legal precedent set by a 1975 court ruling that permits US immigration authorities to engage in racial profiling:

> In *United States v. Brignoni-Ponce*, the Supreme Court sanctioned the use of "apparent Mexican ancestry" as a valid factor in an immigration law enforcement officer's analysis on whether to detain a suspected undocumented immigrant because "[t]he likelihood that any given person of Mexican ancestry is an alien is high enough to make Mexican appearance a relevant factor." Through the years, this ethnic classification has evolved without any explanation in the courts into its current vague and all-encompassing form: "Hispanic

appearance." This unclear and over-generalized ethnic classification is still widely used today by the United States Border Patrol (USBP) in their immigration investigatory stops and upheld on a daily basis by federal courts around the country, especially those courts located in the southern border.[23]

This legal classification of "Hispanic appearance" is an act of criminalizing people of color. It justifies detaining individuals solely based on the color of their skin and their appearance—subjective characteristics dependent upon the assessments and biases of state agents such as Border Patrol with the power to enact violence at will. Chapablanco argues that people of "Hispanic origin and minority groups" should be very concerned about this ruling.

Chapablanco goes on to discuss the legal justifications for being detained, especially while going through a Border Patrol checkpoint when traveling. In the 1976 Supreme Court ruling *United States v. Martinez-Fuerte*, the court held that it was legal to search the vehicles of people passing through highway checkpoints that are stationed less than one hundred miles from the US-Mexico border. The rationalization for this decision was that "reasonable suspicion would be impractical to enforce due to the heavy flow of traffic and because it would not effectively deter the 'well-disguised' operations of smugglers and undocumented immigrants traveling to the interior of the country."[24] Here, we see the court reject the idea of evaluating individuals based on "reasonable suspicion" and instead employing coded language that criminalizes people of color and endorses racial profiling. Including terminology like "smugglers" and "undocumented immigrants" in legal decisions racializes those crossing the border and thus criminalizes brown-skinned people not just at Border Patrol checkpoints but throughout the United States.

In fact, since its inception, the USBP has been granted unlimited jurisdiction to persecute persons who cross the US-Mexico border or whom they perceive to have crossed it, well beyond the border itself. The agency was created in 1924 to patrol the border and prevent illegal crossings. The following year, Congress heard arguments to determine the new agency's authority and granted USBP "broad powers of arrest without a warrant of suspected aliens entering or attempting to enter the country in violation of immigration law."[25] Because the US government attributed any growth of Mexican communities in the borderlands region to illegal immigration, USBP was authorized to patrol, detain, and interrogate any persons whom they perceived to be "illegal." According to Chapablanco, the agency "started using race and ethnicity as an indicator of illegal entry or the individual's immigration status. USBP officers would use the stereotypical profile of the 'Mexican Brown'—'about 5'5" to 5'8"; dark brown hair; brown eyes; dark complexion'—to detain individuals and inquire about their immigration status."[26]

The authority of USBP, (now called CBP) has only grown over the years. Agents are not only legally permitted to interrogate anyone they perceive to fit the profile, as with Rodriguez, but are also able to go into cities in search of undocumented immigrants in order to arrest and detain them. Martínez makes this point in "Driving while Brown," criticizing the ways that money and resources are thrown at Border Patrol with the intent to essentially terrorize Brown and Black communities. She writes, "A continually beefed-up U.S. Border Patrol working with the U.S. military has meant that more of us, particularly people of color, are being stopped and searched in the course of our travels within the United Sates. Not crossing international borders—just driving from point to point inside the country."[27]

Martínez addresses this issue in *Mother Tongue* as well. Sanctuary movement activist María helps refugee José Luis get settled in Old Town Albuquerque, a tourist area of the city, and José Luis gets a job washing dishes at a local restaurant. All too aware of USBP's unlimited jurisdiction, María worries about José Luis's safety traversing the city and keeps an eye on him as he leaves his shift. After work, he often stops to look at the jewelry crafted by the Navajo women sitting nearby, causing María to feel "unnerved." She explains, "The Border Patrol had recently opened an office, declaring

Albuquerque a border town—a city like El Paso or Brownsville, ordered to empty its pockets and produce its documents. I feared if I lost sight of José Luis, the Patrol might take him away in one of its avocado-colored vans. And they could have, easily; they were armed to the teeth."[28]

In highlighting María's concern for José Luis, Martínez emphasizes the racial profiling practices central to agencies like USBP, even in areas far from the US-Mexico border. Albuquerque is approximately 270 miles away. Characterizing it as a "border town" exhibits USBP's—and more recently, ICE's—vast jurisdiction and authority to terrorize people of color wherever they are. As evident in María's fear for José Luis, immigration officials have the power to go to any area with a large Latinx population and perceive those with brown skin as both foreign and criminal. Additionally, since the late 1980s, local police forces in some municipalities have collaborated with federal immigration agencies to pursue individuals and groups they consider "illegal."[29]

Institutionalizing the criminalization of refugees of color has led not only to persecution by US governmental bodies but also media portrayals that villainize them and garner support for such treatment backed by right-wing politicians. Psychology researchers Victoria M. Esses, Stelian Medianu, and Andrea S. Lawson have found that negative depictions of refugees in media outlets cause their dehumanization by the general public. This is especially true when refugees are seen as "bogus queue-jumpers," meaning that they have falsified their asylum claims in order to enter the country. According to Esses, Medianu, and Lawson:

> Such depictions grab the public's attention, alerting them to potential physical, economic, and cultural threats. In this way, uncertainty can be used to media and political advantage, allowing the transformation of relatively mundane episodes into newsworthy events that can be sold to the public and can serve as support for relatively extreme political platforms. The resultant dehumanization of immigrants and refugees may

appeal to members of the public, serving to justify the status quo, strengthening ingroup-outgroup boundaries, and defending against threats to the ingroup's position in society.[30]

Thus, hostile media depictions maintain a climate of general suspicion toward refugees that, due to their racialization, creates a broad threat of violence for Latinx communities in the US.

As a journalist, Martínez knew this all too well. She addresses the media scrutinization of refugees in *Mother Tongue*, when María and José Luis are looking at an article published in the fictitious *Albuquerque Herald* about a speech he had given the night prior. Before reading the article, María warns José Luis about how he will be portrayed: "I said, because your skin is brown, what you say will be followed by words like Romero claimed. Whereas if you were white, it would read, Romero said. That is how they disappear people here. Reporters aim cameras at you like Uzis. They insert notebooks and microphones between themselves and your history."[31] María and José Luis find that the article is indeed filled with language that implicitly fosters suspicion, such as "so-called death squads," "alleged," and "claim," while an immigration supervisor also interviewed is described with more neutral terms like "said." By drawing attention to subtle representations in media that consciously or subconsciously cast doubt on refugees' accounts and take immigration officials' words as fact, Martínez exposes the insidious racism directed toward refugees of color. Shining a light on this and other modes of racialization and criminalization, her work breaks the spell of the official narrative about Central American refugees.

Criminalizing the Sanctuary Movement of the 1980s

Martínez did not only write about the sanctuary movement's work with Central American refugees in the 1980s; she was also an active movement participant. She and other US citizens as well as legal residents mobilized to provide refugees with aid and shelter. In response, the US government turned the violence directed toward refugees onto sanctuary movement activists, subjecting many to surveillance, arrest, and federal criminal charges. In doing so, the United States extended the criminalization of refugees of color to those who helped them as well as to their activist work.

One such activist was John Fife, a Presbyterian minister and sanctuary movement leader in Tucson, Arizona. Fife was actively targeted for his work from 1982 to 1992 when he helped fifteen thousand Central American refugees by giving them a safe place to stay in his church, Southside Presbyterian Church in Tucson. In the introduction to a 2008 interview with Fife published in *Reflections*, a journal issued by Yale Divinity School, the federal government's targeting is explained: "By the mid-1980s, the federal government sent spies into his church to gather evidence against Fife's efforts, and in 1986 he was convicted with seven others on alien-smuggling charges. He served a five-year probation sentence, a turn of events that never interrupted his work as Southside pastor or as activist churchman."[32] Fife is just one of many movement activists who were criminalized, persecuted for simply helping Central American refugees find shelter and food, an act rooted in kindness and altruism.

Martínez worked with Fife in the sanctuary movement and writes about him and his congregation in her memoir. In a chapter titled "A Moment in History," she paints a picture in the reader's mind of a service at his Southside Presbyterian Church where she reads her poetry to "convicted felons, unindicted coconspirators, the not guilty but not necessarily innocent, and refugee activists who'd suffered under brutal dictatorship." She elaborates: "In short, ordinary people who adamantly refused to look the other way. Holiness pervaded the sanctuary proper."[33] Martínez represents the group before her as holy, comprised of people like Christ's disciples: countercultural, radical, and exhibiting love for those in need.

It is fitting that Martínez characterizes these activists as holy. What we now call *sanctuary* has deep roots in Christian tradition. This type of resistance is ancient, forged by individuals and networks seeking to aid those persecuted by hegemonic powers.

According to A. Naomi Paik, the word *sanctuary* has a "genealogy that extends back to the origin stories of Exodus and Jesus, Mary, and Joseph." At its core is the notion of welcoming a foreigner who is fleeing violence. Paik further explains, "The term indicates a site of refuge where the authority of God prevails over the authority of the government . . . civil authorities recognised religious sanctuary as providing temporary refuge for people accused of breaking state laws in the Graeco-Roman and early Christian era, under Roman Catholic law, and under seventeenth-century English common law."[34] Sanctuary goes hand in hand with helping the persecuted, those who unjustly face not only individual somatic violence but also latent violence. In the nineteenth-century United States, the Underground Railroad was a sanctuary, a resistance network that provided shelter, food, and support to enslaved people escaping bondage, even though doing so was both illegal and very dangerous. Government agencies have legally justified deporting refugees fleeing violence and arresting aid workers for having compassion and love for those desperate for safety.

Martínez continues discussing her involvement in the sanctuary movement by recounting an experience in 1986, when she joined Lutheran pastor Reverend Glen Remer-Thamert at the US-Mexico border to aid two pregnant refugees from El Salvador. Martínez and Remer-Thamert traveled to El Paso in August of 1986 and walked across the international bridge to meet the two women. After they crossed into the United States, Martínez and Remer-Thamert drove them from El Paso to Albuquerque. Although she accompanied the pastor as a journalist, Martínez ultimately wrote a poem about the encounter called "Nativity," which is what she read to the group at Southside Presbyterian Church. When Martínez was indicted for conspiracy for aiding an undocumented person, "Nativity" was used as evidence against her in federal court. She only includes two lines from the poem in *Confessions*, lines that she calls "the poem's punchline," which highlight the hypocrisy of right-wing politicians that claim to be Christians following Christ's call to love thy neighbor yet send money to enable Central American countries to kill their own citizens. Below is the poem in its entirety, with the "punchline" italicized:

>Your eyes, large as Canada, welcome
>this stranger.
>We meet in a Juárez train station
>where you sat for hours,
>your offspring blooming in you
>like cactus fruit,
>dresses stained where breasts leak,
>panties in purses tagged
>"Hecho en El Salvador,"
>your belts like equators,
>mark north from south,
>borders I cannot cross,
>for I am an American reporter,
>pen and notebook, the tools
>of my tribe, distance us,
>though in any other era I might
>press a stethoscope to your wounds,
>hear the symphony of the unborn,
>finger forth infants to light,
>wipe afterbirth, cut cords.
>
>*It is impossible to raise a child*
>*in that country.*
>
>Sisters, I am no saint. Just a woman
>who happens to be a reporter,
>a reporter who happens
>to be a woman,
>squat in forest, peeing
>on pine needles,
>watching you vomit morning sickness,
>a sickness infinite as the war in El Salvador,

> a sickness my pen and notebook will not ease,
> tell me, ¿Por qué están aquí?
> How did you cross over?
> *In my country we sing of a baby in a manger,*
> finance death squads,
> how to write of this shame,
> of the children you chose to save?
>
> It is impossible to raise a child
> in that country.
>
> A North American reporter,
> I smile, you tell me you are due
> in December, we nod,
> knowing what women know.
> I shut my notebook,
> watch your car rock
> through the Gila,
> a canoe hanging over the windshield
> like the beak of an eagle,
> babies turning in your wombs,
> summoned to Belén to be born.[35]

The poem shows Martínez wrestling with her privilege as an American reporter and her identity as a woman and a Chicana. She feels connected to the two refugees she is aiding, imagining herself as a *partera*, a midwife, that will deliver the infants in utero at that moment. The connection is primal, instinctive, as Martínez rejects writing about the women as objects to be scrutinized by privileged Americans who have no idea what is going on in El Salvador. In rejecting the role of reporter, Martínez adopts the role of doula, squatting in the forest to urinate alongside the women, supporting them as they face the hardships of coming undocumented into a hostile and racist country. And at the end, Martínez celebrates the life soon to come forth, as the shepherds did when Christ was born in Bethlehem. It is truly a beautiful proclamation of holiness in the righteousness of seeking refuge and giving aid to the refugee.

Conclusion

Latent violence continues to pulse at the US-Mexico border, a violence rooted in the very soil as the US government deploys more and more CBP agents, armed to the teeth, to persecute refugees fleeing for their lives. The US nation-state has constructed a legal system and public narrative that criminalizes refugees of color—refugees who are seeking safety from violence, poverty, and exploitation in their home countries that the US government helped to generate. This state violence is enshrined in law with official distinctions between refugees and asylum seekers, creating a language of criminalization that automatically casts suspicion on certain types of migrants over others, with harsh and heartbreaking consequences.

The literary work of Demetria Martínez illuminates this criminalization and racialization of refugees of color, particularly those fleeing brutal Central American civil wars in the 1980s.

She and other participants in the sanctuary movement were also persecuted for providing aid to refugees in need, some even facing federal charges and jail time. By documenting experiences that challenge the dominant narrative espoused by the US nation-state, her writing contributes to a significant body of cultural production that helps sustain a memory community to preserve knowledge of this state violence—an end to which is nowhere in sight.

CHAPTER FOUR

PRIESTESS Y *PASTORA*

Transnational Female Spiritual Leadership in Ana Castillo's *So Far from God* (1993) and María Amparo Escandón's *Esperanza's Box of Saints* (1998)

Gender roles are a structural violence that mostly manifest in the home, particularly with concepts such as that of the "nuclear family." The nuclear family is defined by two adults, usually a man and a woman in patriarchal societies, and their children. Many feminists, including Chicana feminists, have argued that the centralization of the nuclear family as a building block in a society is crucial to nationalist ideologies and white supremacist ideas in particular, as I will discuss in this chapter. Resistance to the concept of the nuclear family is crucial for Chicana feminists such as Laura E. Pérez, who argues that "for Chicanas/os, 'nation' is made to signify differently, and symbolic language is made to course through alternative venues than the ones imagined, colonized, legitimized by the order that denies oppressed peoples access to its center of articulation."[1] The transnational nature of Chicanx identity, with its ties to Mexico and the United States, allows an imagining of citizenship in a transgressive, liminal light: *ni de aquí, ni de allá*. Moreover, Chicanx, as well as other racialized groups, experience systemic oppression through racial and gendered violence that manifest in the nuclear family, as well as those who are outside the parameters of the nuclear family, such as single parents, queer couples, and undocumented or mixed-status families. This is the structural violence that Galtung articulates in his conceptualization of violence in which at the societal level there is a limiting of a specific group of people's potential, in this case that of racialized women and queer persons who are subjected to existing within prescribed parameters that do not threaten the imagined community of a nation. When existing outside these prescribed parameters of the heteronormative nuclear family, the violence they experience—be it through domestic violence, kidnapping, and human trafficking, as will be discussed in this chapter—is ultimately justified by blaming the victims.

These are the themes I will explore in this chapter through my analysis of literary representations of Chicana mothers subverting the gender roles prescribed in a patriarchal heteronormative society. These subversive female figures are incredibly powerful, especially when considering that they are being subversive in religious and spiritual contexts. Specifically, the subversive representation of women of color in Ana Castillo's *So Far from God* (1993) and María Amparo Escandón's *Esperanza's Box of Saints* (1999), Chicanas and Mexicanas in this case, in religious leadership roles in their homes and communities dismantles the gender roles enforced by the patriarchal concept of the nuclear family, thus a borderland consciousness is present in these Chicanx/Mexicanx homes.

Borderlands consciousness is manifest through what Gloria Anzaldúa describes as breaking with traditions that oppress Chicanas and Chicanos by uplifting a praxis of "[botando] lo que no vale," or "throwing away" what does not have value in our culture.[2] Anzaldúa, in effect, prescribes a borderlands consciousness which the protagonists, Sofia in *So Far from God* and Esperanza in *Esperanza's Box of Saints*, apply by "throwing away" the patriarchal aspects of the Christian religion by embracing their own spiritual authority. The protagonist women in both novels gain spiritual authority through their role as mothers and actively utilize their motherhood to enter into roles and spaces deemed only for men, both religiously and culturally. These protagonists subvert the dominant and patriarchal structures of the church and the heteronormative nuclear family by claiming the roles of priestess and *pastora* (pastor)—what I read as enactments of their agency and Chicana feminist praxis. These actions, in turn, reposition what I call "La Madre" from an idealized figure of submission to a powerful figure of spiritual authority in her home and community, which she then uses to determine the religiosity and spiritual expression that dignifies her children through decolonial love. By examining the literary work of Castillo, a Chicana writer, and Escandón, a feminist Mexicana writer who was born in Mexico City and moved to the United States in adulthood, I will analyze representations of the mother that emphasize spiritual authority in each protagonist's home and borderlands community. As women of color who face transnational and global issues that harm their children, Sofia and Esperanza determine their religiosity and take hold of their spiritual authority. They gain a borderlands consciousness to dignify their children rather than abide by patriarchal religious institutions for guidance on spiritual matters.

The novels written by Castillo and Escandón reveal how the figure of La Madre crosses national boundaries and challenges any notion of borders; she's a transnational subject who defies hegemonic notions of citizenship. Sofia, a Nuevomexicana, and Esperanza, a Mexicana, are women of color and Las Madres who face global issues that harm their children. In other words, their subjectivities and struggles are similar despite the physical border that separates them. These transnational maternal representations "throw away" and break with oppressive traditions, and demonstrate that mothers are the spiritual leaders of the home space and the community. This chapter establishes that the La Madre figure is portrayed as a leader who protects and guides her children as well as members of her community; serves as an intermediary between that which is secular and that which is sacred; and transgresses borders that are represented in both novels. These actions occur through the spiritual leadership of the La Madre as a priestess and as a pastora.

The Spiritual Authority of La Madre

Sofia and Esperanza's spiritual authority manifests in a variety of ways; however, the literal decentering of male religious authority occurs in two specific and parallel scenes. In these scenes, Sofia and Esperanza gain authority in different ways that result in recentering Brown mothers that theologize with male Catholic priests about the nature of the miraculous reappearances of their daughters after death.[3] In *So Far from God*, Sofia's youngest daughter dies and resurrects during the funeral. When the child awakens, she flies from her coffin to the top of the church roof. Father Jerome inserts himself into the scene, attempting to decipher the nature of this supernatural occurrence by asking the child, "Is this an act of God or of Satan that brings you back to us, that has flown you up to the roof like a bird? Are you the devil's messenger or a winged angel?"[4] Sofia, a grieving mother that is done with her role of a palatable self-sacrificing mother, confronts Father Jerome:

> "Don't you dare!" she screamed at Father Jerome, charging at him and beating him with her fists. "Don't you dare start this about *my* baby! If our Lord in His heaven has sent my child back to me, don't you dare start this backward thinking against her; the devil does not produce miracles! And *this* is a miracle, an answer to the prayers of a brokenhearted mother, ¡hombre necio, pendejo . . . !"[5]

Sofia confronts Father Jerome's theology of miracles and articulates her own theology that declares La Loca's resurrection a miracle. This declaration is an act that defies patriarchal norms because it is usually Vatican officials who can declare miracles. Sofia theologizes to dignify her daughter's supernatural resurrection by confronting the priest; she defends the well-being of her daughter against "backward thinking" that will inevitably harm her daughter, even as she was nicknamed "La Loca" after this supernatural occurrence by the community as she refused human contact by anyone other than her mother.

Similarly, Esperanza confronts Father Salvador's imposition on her search for her missing daughter, Blanca, after an apparition of Saint Judas Thaddeus (or San Judas Tadeo as he is known in Mexico) on Esperanza's dirty stove tells her that Blanca is not dead.

Esperanza goes on to exhume Blanca's coffin to find that it is indeed empty, and she commences a search of brothels that extend from Tlacotalpán, her hometown in Veracruz, to the US-Mexico border town of Tijuana, and then across the border illegally to Los Angeles. Esperanza's transnational search to the United States borderlands leads her back home to Tlacotalpán. While taking a bath, she hears Blanca's voice and sees her in a rusty stain: "In that stain, I saw Blanca's face. She was wearing a beautiful Jarocha costume. She said, 'Mommy, you and me, we'll always be together.'"[6] Anticipating Father Salvador's disbelief, Esperanza goes on to theologize the nature of this miraculous apparition, even when he questions if she will notify the Vatican:

> Father, do you understand? I finally know what San Judas Tadeo meant. Blanca is not dead. Blanca is not alive. She is that little space in between. That's where I was supposed to look for her. . . . Blanca's apparitions are not important to the rest of the world. Why do you think she's appearing before me on my bathroom wall and not before the whole town on the bridge wall moss, like San Juan Nepomuceno did six years ago? This is just between the two of us. She's my own little saint, my little *santita*. So, please don't start paperwork.[7]

Esperanza experiences the sanctification of her daughter Blanca, whom she interprets as neither dead nor alive. The miracle of Blanca's sanctification could have only happened with Esperanza's fierce search for her daughter in the face of the mystery of Blanca's empty coffin. Instead of going to the priest to ask for an interpretation of the miracle, Blanca gives the priest her own theological interpretation and declares that Blanca's apparition is between herself and Blanca. Sofia and Esperanza experience the death of their young daughters as well as the miraculous apparitions of these daughters after death. As the spiritual authorities of their homes, Sofia and Esperanza are the protectors of their daughter's souls and thus assert their authority by theologizing with the priests regarding the nature of the miracles of their daughters' coming back from the dead. Their spiritual authority is a transgressive crossing of gender roles that serves as a vehicle for social change, and this is possible through their roles as mothers dignifying their children's existence.

Transnational Chicana Feminism in the Spiritual Authority of La Madre

Transgressive crossings such as crossing the US-Mexico border (whether undocumented or by seeking asylum), crossing into the workforce as a woman, or crossing the patriarchal parameters of religious authority are all feminist acts that subvert the nation-state's parameters of citizenship. Norma Alarcón, Caren Kaplan, and Minoo Moallem discuss that "the nation-state sharpens the defining lines of citizenship for women, racialized ethnicities, and sexualities in the construction of a socially stratified society."[8] To continue the project of nation-building, the nuclear family is thus crucial for the reproduction of the citizenry, but only within the parameters of the ideal citizen in accordance with how hegemonic groups define it. The creation of borders and a continued rhetoric in support of the maintenance of borders is thus necessary, as both determine the Other, the foreigner, the noncitizen. Alarcón, Kaplan, and Moallem present a "communal identity crisis" in which the parameters of citizenship are disrupted by racial and sexual determinants: "At the core of the modern nation-state, a contradiction is set in motion insofar as there is denial of sexual or racial difference or both, and simultaneous universalization of difference."[9] The significance of religion comes into play as it creates a universalization of what a nuclear family ought to look like: one which is based on patriarchal Christian tradition with the composition of the family as husband, wife, and children. This structure in turn leads to the ways women's bodies are "bordered" based on male perceptions. Chandra Mohanty describes this bordering of women's bodies when she says, "Borders suggest both containment and safety, and women often pay the price for daring to claim integrity, security, and safety of our bodies and living spaces."[10] Indeed, when women do not subscribe to heteronormative notions of family structures, or their circumstances have brought them to exist on their own without a male presence, they become the leaders and authorities of their nuclear family, which disrupts and causes a communal identity crisis that shakes the established borders and parameters as defined by hegemonic institutions. An act of defiance against patriarchal Christian notions of family is thus an act of defiance toward the parameters of citizenship. Chicana feminist praxis, as represented by Sofia and Esperanza's mothering, decenters male headship of the family structure and challenges these parameters of citizenship at the individual and familial level.

The concept of the nuclear family is a microcosm of global issues that reach beyond nation-states' borders, as they demonstrate capitalist transnational power structures. This point is echoed in Leigh Johnson's discussion of how Chicana literary characters in the novels *Black Widow's Wardrobe* (1999) by Lucha Corpi and *Mother Tongue* (1994) by Demetria Martínez are "global citizens." Johnson argues that the nature of the characters' narrative arc is transnational because there exists an "inability of any novel to so stay contained within the hemisphere."[11] As transnational and Chicana feminist texts, Castillo's and Escandón's novels feature characters who defy notions of citizenship as dictated by American as well as Mexican patriarchal power structures. The women also decenter white male power—those who are typically the actors—and in turn recenter Brown mothers to determine family structures. Castillo's and Escandón's protagonists achieve this through religious authority as Las Madres within their homes and family structures, particularly when racist, sexist, and homophobic violence affects their daughters. The importance of mothers of color enacting social change for their children is one of the main points of Johnson's analysis of transnational Chicana feminist representations in Chicana literature: "Motherwork can be concentrated on one family, one community, but more frequently, it reverberates through communities to produce social change."[12]

Transnational Violence Presented in *So Far from God* and *Esperanza's Box of Saints*

In the world outside of Sofia and Esperanza's homes, hegemonic forces represented through neoliberal ideologies and racist and homophobic politics enforce a patriarchy that rejects the woman. These forces are represented in the novels as responsible for harming and destroying these women's daughters. The maintenance of the ideal citizen is a form of policing the borders of a body politic. Identities that are queer, nonwhite, poor, and nonevangelical are deemed causes of the previously mentioned communal identity crisis. The violence perpetuated against those who are deemed Other are thus targeted in a variety of ways. In *So Far from God*, while Sofi's daughter Caridad, who was initially characterized as an overly sexual hetero woman, finds true love with a woman named Esmeralda, she commits suicide after a Penitente who was in love with Caridad rapes Esmeralda in a jealous rage.[13] While she ultimately falls in love with a woman, Caridad's sexuality was transgressive from the beginning of the novel, because even though she had sexual relations with men, she was still seen as a *puta* for embracing her sexuality. A second daughter of Sofi, Fe, develops cancer while working in the Acme International factory in her attempt to assimilate to US dominant culture. Seeking career success as a journalist brought another of Sofi's daughters, Esperanza, an untimely death, as she was assigned to covering the war in the Middle East and killed in a conflict zone. And even Sofi's baby, La Loca, the daughter that never left home, inexplicably contracts AIDS and, at the end of the novel, also dies.

Each of the daughter's deaths are stark reminders of the ways capitalist systems that monetize all things do so on a global scale that targets the Other. In her 1999 essay "Chicana Feminism: In the Tracks of 'The' Native Woman," Norma Alarcón discusses the notion of how women of color, in this case Mexican and Chicana women with Indigenous roots, are seen as wild or "'non-civilized' dark" women. She argues that while the Brownness of women includes them in Mexico under the national identity of mestizaje, in the United States the Brown woman is othered through notions of white supremacy and therefore deemed wild. Alarcón concludes that Brown women are then "often compelled to acquiesce with the 'civilizing' new order in male terms."[14] Attachment to men therefore brings Brown women into the acceptable terms of belonging to enter into the body politic as a member of society. Being an independent Brown woman, on the other hand, is deemed taboo; an independent Brown woman is a target due to her perceived vulnerability.

In *Esperanza's Box of Saints*, Esperanza is precisely this independent Brown woman: she is a young widow that lives with her only daughter, Blanca, and her friend Soledad. After the apparition of San Judas Tadeo, Esperanza traverses dangerous spaces in search of her daughter. Among them is the cemetery where she exhumes Blanca's coffin to confirm that she had, in fact, died. Instead, she finds that Blanca may have possibly been kidnapped and is now being sex trafficked.[15] A 2022 United Nations report on human trafficking worldwide finds that from data collected in 2020 (which is the most recent), there were 51,580 detected victims of trafficking in 166 countries. Of these detected victims, 42 percent were women, 23 percent were men, 18 percent were girls, and 17 percent were boys. Also, of these detected victims, 38.8 percent of the victims were trafficked for forced labor, 38.7 percent for sexual exploitation, 10.3 percent for "mixed forms of exploitation" (a mix of forced labor and sexual exploitation), 10.2 percent for forced criminal activity, 0.9 percent for forced marriages, 0.7 percent for exploitative begging, 0.3 percent for illegal adoption, and 0.2 percent for removal of organs. And while the COVID-19 pandemic caused a 11 percent decrease in victims detected from 2019 to 2020, in North America the numbers of female victims increased 24 percent and male victims also increased by 11 percent. The numbers are worse for Central and South America, with an increase of 38 percent from 2019 to 2020 for male victims. Additionally, the UN report cautions that the decrease in the number of detected victims during the pandemic may be misleading. According to the UN report, before the pandemic, sexual exploitation reportedly happened in spaces such as nightclubs and bars, but researchers hypothesize that due to mitigation of the spread of the virus, sexual exploitation is probably now moved to "less visible and less safe locations, making this form of trafficking more concealed and harder to be detected."[16] Thus, even with a deadly infectious virus causing a global pandemic that halted most economic activity, trafficking of persons continued, became more pervasive as it went underground, and even increased in certain countries. The depravity of this illegal industry is scary and real.

In the novel, Esperanza, although in a small town in Veracruz, is well aware of the world's sexual depravity and how her daughter could have become a victim of its utter violence. Father Salvador describes her drive to find her daughter as "unstoppable": "She's on a mission. It's [God's] will. All I can do is pray for her. Am I wrong to believe her?"[17] The targeting of women deemed vulnerable due to lack of male presence is not by accident. Justifications for sex that include women "being in the wrong place at the wrong time" perpetuate parameters of ideal citizenry determined by male presence, sponsorship, and protection. Thus, the motherwork, and in this case spiritual authority, is powerful as it takes an idealized notion of womanhood—motherhood—and utilizes it to counter the bordering and policing of women's bodies. La Madre goes into dark and dangerous places and brings her child home to heal, regardless of the expectations of what a society, a nation-state and its borders, and policing deem illegitimate about her and her child.

Defiance and Transgression of La Madre's Spiritual Authority and Leadership

This chapter conceptualizes La Madre as a literary representation of religious authority—a controversial idea within Chicanx culture. In Mexico and the American Southwest, religious teachings mainly derive from the Catholic Church. This religious institution has influenced acceptable gendered behaviors with strong foundations in Catholic theology.[18] Culturally speaking, women have only been able to take on the role of the teacher when it comes to religious instruction. The irony is that while teaching children religious doctrine is expected, women are not permitted to have any kind of leadership role within the church. For example, the Catholic Church still does not allow women to become priests.[19] The Vatican has justified women's exclusion from these leadership roles with the dogma of complementarity—the theological teaching that women and men were created as complements of one another, each given a different role by God. In *When Women Become Priests: The Catholic Women's Ordination Debate*, Kelley A. Raab explains, "Complementarity refers to the idea that men and women have different roles to perform within church and society, originating from innate, predetermined functions. In this 'two nature' vision of humanity, men and women are ordained to complement one another, leading to a division of male and female roles, which are not interchangeable."[20] One of the "roles that [is] not interchangeable" is leadership within the church or home. While the woman complements the man in her procreative capacity and thus aids in augmenting the number of Catholics in the "Reign of God," according to doctrine, she will never be able to become a priest or have headship of the home, which is a supposed role of the man.

Raab's research includes an investigation of official Vatican documents, which she uses to clarify the theological explanations preventing women from becoming priests.[21] She divides her findings into three justifications: tradition, the male biological or "natural" resemblance to Jesus Christ, and the biblical allegory depicting Christ as the bridegroom and the church as the bride. The first justification of tradition is not insignificant: in the Roman Catholic Church, tradition carries the same doctrinal weight as scripture. A 1976 Vatican declaration directly addressing the "Question of Admission of Women to the Ministerial Priesthood" indicates that traditionally, a woman has never been named to the priesthood. Additionally, explanations regarding men's natural resemblance to Jesus Christ and the image of the bridegroom and bride demonstrate a direct intention of subjugating women according to the doctrine of complementarity. Considering the 1976 declaration, Raab asserts, "The document states that the incarnation took place in the form of the male sex and that this fact cannot be disassociated from the doctrine of salvation. Fundamentally, the argument runs, Christ cannot be symbolized as a woman because the historical Jesus was not a woman."[22]

The Vatican emphasizes Jesus's sex to justify preventing women from entering the priesthood. Raab defines this rationale as "biological determinism," a concept established by Thomas Aquinas in *Summa Theologica* (1485).[23] Aquinas declared, "Because the female sex cannot signify eminence of rank—women being in a state of subjection—it follows that she cannot receive the sacrament of orders."[24] This Thomist belief has had repercussions affecting women's participation in the Catholic Church to this day. Sofia and Esperanza directly transgress this idea of biological determinism with the simple fact that they are female and they establish their religious authority over Father Jerome and Father Salvador.

The influence of Catholicism and its dogma of complementarity within Chicanx culture affected relationships between women and men during the Chicano movement in the 1960s and 1970s. Tenets of cultural nationalism at the center of the movement emphasized a romanticized notion of the family because Chicanos wanted to embrace Mexican culture and reject the dominant culture of the United States. Denise Segura and Beatriz Pesquera explain that this idealization of the family is an empowering tool for activists who support Chicano cultural nationalism: "Politically, cultural nationalism called for self-determination including the maintenance of Mexican cultural patterns, culturally relevant education, and community control of social institutions."[25] However, the maintenance of "Mexican cultural patterns" turned the family into a romanticized concept, which had consequences for the ways that male activists treated women. Many Chicanos had no interest in listening to Chicana activists who denounced sexism and sexual harassment, and effectively marginalized them within the movement. As Segura and Pesquera explain, "Chicanas who deviated from a nationalist political stance were subjected to many negative sanctions including being labeled *vendidas* (sell-outs), or *agabachadas* (white identified). Once labeled thus, they became subject to marginalization within Chicano Movement organizations."[26] Calling these Chicanas *vendidas* and *agabachadas* was a way to control them and maintain traditional notions of family that were both patriarchal and sexist. One of these traditions was women's submission to male authority, designed to maintain complementarity within the family. Due to these conflicts, Chicana feminists started their own liberation movement with art, literature, intellectualism, and queer sexuality that subverted the notion that women must submit to men.

One way that Chicana feminists attempted to undermine such ideas in the 1970s was to appropriate the concept of La Madre—to decolonize her and rid her of patriarchal ties. Chicana feminists have written, painted, and represented the mother figure in ways that continue to decolonize La Madre as well as all Chicanas. Artists' and writers' creativity throughout the 1970s and 1980s has allowed future Chicanas to create religious representations of the mother figure that include different religious expressions—artistic production that continues to this day. Gloria Anzaldúa discusses the importance of La Madre in relation to Chicanx identity in articulating the three mothers of Chicanas/os: Malinche, La Llorona, and Guadalupe. According to Anzaldúa, "the *virgen*/whore dichotomy" pits Guadalupe against Malinche and La Llorona, with Guadalupe as the *virgen*—that is, the ideal example of Chicana/Mexicana womanhood that fits well within the borders of the ideal woman citizen—and Malinche and La Llorona as the whores.[27] However, like Anzaldúa, other Chicana feminists have reappropriated the figure of Malinche and La Llorona to demonstrate transgressive Chicana motherhood that embraces sexuality and agency and breaks barriers.[28] Castillo and Escandón depict the Chicana/Mexicana mother as the practitioner of decolonial love, which is the vehicle by which the mother is or becomes a spiritual authority, therefore providing a sacred place for her children to heal and transcend systems of patriarchy, racism, and capitalist globalism that are so damaging and violent toward people of color.

Castillo deliberately writes the mother character of Sofia to go against these nationalist ideals of Chicana motherhood. Melissa Schoeffel explains:

> Rather than focusing on how motherhood threatens a woman's individual autonomy, her [Castillo's] focus is on how the cultural idealization of motherhood is always paired with the denigration of actual mothers, and that such a paradox is the patriarchy's response to the (re)creative power of women evidenced in the physical and cultural work of mothers.... Reclaiming motherhood—which means recognizing the political effects of its ideologies—is for Castillo an essential step in imagining "truly nurturing society," one that does not idealize or denigrate mothers but, rather uses maternal practices as models for ethical social relations.[29]

It is through this reclaiming of motherhood that Castillo and Escandón explore how La Madre is a source of social transformation through Sofia's and Esperanza's transgressive roles as spiritual authority figures. Sofia functions as a priestess of her temple, which is her home, and Esperanza functions as a pastora and journeys across the US-Mexico borderlands. These roles are intended to dignify their children's lives while at the same time legitimizing their leadership in the face of hardship and their agency in matters of sexuality and political identity.

As priestess in her home/temple, Sofia evokes animal sacrifices for the good of the congregation (her children)—a motif that most vividly encapsulates her role as a priestess. In the novel, "Sofi single-handedly ran the Carne Buena Carnecería she inherited from her parents. She raised most of the livestock that she herself (with the help of La Loca) butchered for the store, managed all its finances, and ran the house on her own to boot."[30] The blood and sacrifice of the animals sold in Sofia's butcher shop support her home/temple, mirroring temples in other religions that ritualized the sacrifice of animals. Throughout the novel, La Loca manifests supernatural healing powers but, as she is inseparable from her mother, La Loca also manifests the spiritual power of the home. Even so, Sofia is the one with the authority to allow others to enter into this sacred space. Only Sofia can touch La Loca because she is the priestess; she is the intermediary between the divine power, the community, and most importantly her daughters who are in need of healing and protection. Castillo's borderlands consciousness is represented throughout the novel in the miracles that occur in Sofia's home/temple because they impact the lives of Sofia's daughters and the community that surrounds them. She creates social change in the community of Tomé when she runs for mayor, even though the town does not offer such a position. Nevertheless, with her candidacy, Sofia gains the trust and respect of the community. This is empowering for women of color.

However, Sofia and her daughters suffered long before this transformation took place. Each daughter (with the exception of La Loca) goes out into the world and comes back to find Sofia's home/temple damaged. While the example of Caridad depicts physical violence, the other daughters face emotional harm and physical, or somatic, violence as well. Out of all of Sofia's daughters, Fe is the one who most desires to assimilate into American society. She seeks the American dream—getting married, having children, and buying a house—and seems to be on the path to achieve it. However, everything changes when Tom, her fiancé, breaks off their engagement. Fe reacts very strangely, as she begins to scream and does not stop. This incident happens around the same time as Caridad is brutally attacked by *la malogra*, an evil monster that originates in New Mexican folk tales, and as a result both sisters are home, hurt, and recovering while La Loca prays for them and Sofia looks after the well-being of the home.[31] This goes on for several months. Then one day, all of a sudden, Caridad's mauled body is miraculously restored to its original state before being destroyed by la malogra, and Fe stops screaming. The differential consciousness is manifested in this miracle; as the older sister, Esperanza, perceives it, "Caridad's and Fe's spontaneous recoveries were beyond all rhyme and reason for anyone."[32] Moreover, this differential consciousness of the miracle in Sofia's home results in decolonial love and is the rupture in Esperanza's logic, as she is the intellectual daughter of the family.

By studying at the university, Esperanza becomes an atheist and develops a cynical attitude toward religion. However, her sisters' tragic experiences motivate Esperanza to search for understanding of what is happening in her mother's home: "She read everything she could find on dysfunctional families, certain now that some of her personal sense of displacement in society had to do with her upbringing. But nowhere did she find anything near to the description of her family."[33] Esperanza is unable to find logic in her sisters' healing. Her intellectualism prevents her from seeing that her home, the temple of Sofia the priestess, is a sacred place that activates Caridad and Fe's recovery. La Loca, being the healing power, prays for her sisters: "She also prayed for [Fe], since that was La Loca's principal reason for being alive, as both her mother and she well knew."[34] But although La Loca represents the healing power of the home, the healing cannot occur without Sofia, the priestess. Sofia, flustered by her two daughters' precarious conditions, suffers a nervous breakdown in the presence of Esperanza. Even with her lack of faith—which reflects Western society's emphasis on logic, scientific thought, and scorn for human strength and the supernatural—Esperanza begs Sofia to not be overcome by her circumstances. It is precisely in these inexplicable cases that rupture exists, encouraging those present to consider a third space, a spiritual world, where everything is possible.

On the surface, the ultimate death of her children may be a blow to Sofia's decolonial love. However, Castillo writes into the narrative several border crossings that are miraculous acts of differential consciousness: these are the border crossings from death to life, from despair to healing and remembrance. These border crossings are La Loca's resurrection when she was a child and Esperanza's spirit coming back to visit Sofia's home. During both of these events, Sofia, along with the Tomé community, witnesses the transcendence of women of color despite what patriarchal and hegemonic systems dictate are their destinies. The paradox of these miraculous events is that they are tragic yet produce hope: it is dignity manifested through the transcendence of border communities over the border that ultimately separates families, and death is the miracle through which Sofia's daughters overcome racial and sexual violence. At the same time, Sofia's temple and priesthood—those spaces and roles not established in religious institutions—provide the place where this transcendence takes place. Castillo beautifully weaves this narrative of unfettering faith and love of the La Madre that bursts through the very terminal concept of death.

Escandón similarly utilizes the transcendence of decolonial love to create a transnational narrative. In *Esperanza's Box of Saints*, Esperanza leaves home to look for her daughter Blanca, thus performing the role of the pastora. Biblical narratives represent this figure as someone who tends a flock of sheep, which includes going out in search of those who are lost. The mother-pastora's transgression also conflicts with the Catholic dogma of complementarity. With her call to go out into the world to care for the flock and search for lost sheep, she challenges the designation of the man as shepherd, or pastor. Miguel de Cervantes's most famous novel, *El Ingenioso Hidalgo Don Quijote de la Mancha* (1605), provides an example of a woman vilified for being a pastora. The character of Marcela is a young woman who wishes to be a pastora and to enjoy the solitude of the land. She is blamed for the death of Grisóstomo, a shepherd who has fallen madly in love with her. Don Quijote and Sancho Panza encounter the procession of mourning for Grisóstomo and, by inquiring about the deceased, are informed that an "endiablada moza" (a young woman possessed by a demon) rejected him, thus causing his tragic death. Regardless, Marcela appears during the funeral to defend herself, saying, "No todas las hermosuras enamoran. . . . Yo nací libre, y para poder vivir libre escogí la soledad de los campos. . . . Tengo libre condición y no gusto de sujetarme. Ni quiero ni aborrezco a nadie."[35] Because Marcela is a pastora, the men around her feel justified in dehumanizing her, as she has entered into male space. In this way, Marcela's transgression, in addition to not reciprocating Grisóstomo's love, is to be bold enough to step outside the home space and find her calling as a pastora. As this example demonstrates, going out into the world, as Marcela did, constitutes subverting the virgin/whore dichotomy and is thus the most transgressive role discussed in this chapter.

Esperanza's faith is so strong that she believes the apparition and throughout the novel does everything in her power to find Blanca. She believes that her daughter is not dead but rather has been kidnapped and made a victim of sex trafficking, leading her investigation to brothels in Tijuana and Los Angeles. Esperanza is not afraid to enter these incredibly dangerous places in order to find her daughter, mirroring the proverbial shepherd, or pastor, in search of their lost sheep. The mother-pastora as a figure of spiritual leadership is the most transgressive of the two representations because of her calling to leave the home space. According to patriarchal customs, the home is the designated space for a woman and in leaving it she may be considered a "public woman"—that is, sexually immoral. As a mother in search of her children, the mother-pastora can be a representation of the multifaceted figure of La Llorona—a woman who, depending on differing versions of the legend, drowns her children in a fit of rage after being betrayed by her beloved or because she was protecting her children from violence and endlessly wanders bodies of water, weeping.[36] Significantly, both La Llorona and the mother-pastora can be characterized as transgressors for rejecting the submission and abnegation expected of a mother in mourning; instead, they look for their children that society has determined are dead.

Sacred Places and Spaces through Chicana Transnational Feminist Motherwork

La Madre has to carve out sacred places and spaces for her children in light of the violence perpetuated against them. Sofia's home and Esperanza's holy journey are spaces and places that are sanctuaries that dignify the existence of their children. The representation of the home as a refuge is a leitmotiv in literature as well as art. However, this leitmotiv resonates more profoundly with people of color due to the violence and oppression of the world outside the home. This idea is reflected in the way that Black feminist author bell hooks describes her grandmother's home in *Yearning: Race, Gender, and Cultural Politics* (1990):

> I speak of this journey as leading to my grandmother's house, even though our grandfather lived there too. In our young minds houses belonged to women, were their special domain, not as property, but as places where all that truly mattered in life took place; the warmth and comfort of shelter, the feeding of our bodies, the nurturing of our souls. There we learned dignity, integrity of being; there we learned to have faith.[37]

This understanding of the home as a refuge is crucial in considering Castillo's novel *So Far from God*, as Castillo similarly emphasizes the home space as fundamental for the well-being, development, and survival of people of color.

Sofia's home, which is located in Tomé, New Mexico, and thus in the US-Mexico borderlands, is a manifestation of Castillo's differential consciousness: this little house is a space in which a mestiza has the power to decolonize her daughters. Sofia functions as a mother-priestess in her domestic space to maintain, as hooks states, the characters' dignity. In his article "Priests and Priestesses in Prehistoric Europe," Johannes Maringer discusses the characteristics and functions of a male (or female) priest. According to Maringer, institutionalized religions define the priest as the person in charge of the spiritual affairs of the community. The priest spreads religious teachings and looks after the physical structure of the temple or church, while the institution he represents assures his well-being. In addition to religious institutional authority, a sense of divine authority is also bestowed upon the priest. As Maringer clarifies, "Their specific character consists of being invested by a community as supernaturally authorized mediators to the transcendental world for the performance of the public cult."[38] Thus, the role of priesthood is assigned by a supernatural entity.

This home, Sofia's temple, is important to her daughters' welfare and serves as a refuge and sacred place. The decolonial love that Sofia manifests in her home represents a parting and entering point, as is the state of Coatlicue, where the physical, emotional, and psychological violence toward the mestiza woman has no power. In addition, the home's healing and refuge is an example of the rupture of "whatever controls in order to find 'understanding and community.'"[39] Kathryn A. Rabuzzi explores this theme in *The Sacred and the Feminine: Toward a Theology of Housework* (1982), arguing that the home, like the church, provides a refuge from the world and thus can be described as a sacred place.[40] Considering the etymology of the word *home*, Rabuzzi determines that in ancient texts written in Hebrew and Greek no such word exists. She only finds the word for *house*, the physical structure.[41]

Rabuzzi also touches on the designation of a place as sacred. She explains that a "space" transforms into a "place" when it holds emotional significance. A place, representing emotional connections, requires a transformation from its inhabitants; that is to say that whether a religious building, home, or landmark, it becomes a place rather than a space because of the value, emotional experience, and history the devout give it.[42] When a place—the home in this case—is appointed as sacred, the transformation of its inhabitants reaches an even more intense level. It is important to observe two things in this process: the purpose of this place and the experience of those who enter into this place. Sofia's home in *So Far from God* is a literary expression of a sacred place. As Doña Felicia declares after a demonic animal, la malogra, ferociously attacks Caridad, "All they did at the hospital was patch you up and send you home, more dead than alive. It was with the help of God, heaven knows how He watches over that house where you come from."[43] Because Sofia's home is a place of sanctuary, it is a temple and Sofia is its priestess, given the task to sanctify this place for the refuge and healing of her community: her daughters. That is the purpose of Sofia's home.

Those who enter are astonished by the miracles that occur there. There is also something to be said about how this sacred place, Sofia's home, is in a space deemed dangerous by its location within the pejorative Wild West, the US-Mexico borderlands: a space vilified by racist representations in media and by politicians is in fact a healing, sacred place for the people of color in these communities.

Another function of Sofia as a priestess in her home is her rejection of those who disturb the sacredness of the place. Sofia's husband, Domingo, is a gambler, and due to his addiction, he abandons his family and home. Sofia does not see him again for years, until he unexpectedly appears one day. Although she is still angry, Sofia forgives Domingo and allows him to come back home. There are moments when it seems that they have reconciled, but Domingo soon goes back to his old gambling ways and ultimately bets the house and loses. It is when Domingo loses the house that Sofia finally divorces him. She forgives him for abandoning and neglecting his daughters but cannot forgive his losing the sacred place that has served as their refuge.

Taking control of her home while caring for her daughters empowers Sofia as a leader. However, when she cannot protect her daughters, she decides to take her leadership beyond her home and into her community. She and a friend plan a campaign to elect Sofia as mayor of Tomé. Her friend, resisting the idea at first, tells Sofia that her imagination is too big, but Sofia responds, "It's not 'imagination' that I've always had, comadre, it's faith! Faith has kept me going."[44] Although their campaign does not result in Sofia's election to office, she and her friend initiate community meetings and debates to determine how to turn Tomé into an economically self-sufficient district. They form Los Ganados y Lana Cooperative, a cooperative that collects wool from community members' sheep. Although Sofia cannot heal Esperanza or La Loca in her home/temple and their deaths cause Sofia unbearable pain, losing Esperanza brings forth an oppositional consciousness in the community that allows them to conceive of a collective effort for self-sufficiency.

In *Esperanza's Box of Saints*, Esperanza ventures outside

the home and sacred space, which leads her across the US-Mexico borderlands. Esperanza's investigation into Blanca's disappearance also leads her to the brothels of Tijuana, where she poses as a sex worker. After discovering her daughter's empty coffin, Saint Judas appears to her two more times, insisting that she continue to search for Blanca. At the suggestion of Father Salvador, Esperanza begins her journey at La Curva, a well-known hotel where sex workers and their patrons meet. It is there that Esperanza determines that her daughter has become a victim of sex trafficking: "I've heard there are people who kidnap girls and sell them to houses of sin."[45] In the novel, Escandón depicts the mother's differential consciousness through acts of entering and leaving these transgressive spaces. Chela Sandoval explains that decolonial love also manifests in what Roland Barthes calls "drifting": "The movement of meanings that will not be governed; it is the intractable itself as it permeates through, in, and outside of power."[46] In addition to entering these transgressive spaces of prostitution and sex trafficking, Esperanza poses as a sex worker—a transgressive act "outside of power"—in order to find her daughter. Moreover, Escandón emphasizes that Esperanza never has sexual relations with her clients, adding to the miraculous nature of her journey. Her encounters with sexual predators like Cacomixtle demonstrate her unyielding will to enter immoral and dangerous spaces and pass as a sex worker. In one of the brothels, Esperanza meets Mr. Scott Haynes, a judge from San Diego, California, with whom she has an intimate relationship. This relationship enables her to enter the United States, as Haynes signs her visa, and thus allows her to continue her search.

Along this journey, Esperanza is steadfast in her spirituality. In the moments when she steps outside of her sex worker pretense, she prays continuously and looks for opportunities for Saint Judas to appear to her again as he does at the beginning of the novel. In addition, because of entering transgressive spaces, Esperanza frequently feels compelled to confess, which she does over the phone with Father Salvador, the priest in the church back in Veracruz. Although she has committed no sin, her descriptions of her journey awaken an intense lust in the priest, as Esperanza reminds him of a sexual relationship he had when he was young. Father Salvador's lust represents the subversion, or recentering, of another binary: male confessor / female confessant. In this case, the person who listens to the confession, Father Salvador, is the one who sins, rather than the person who confesses, Esperanza. The recentering of Esperanza as pure and free of sin leads Father Salvador, as well as Scott Haynes, to acknowledge their own male power and privilege as they take advantage of Esperanza's innocence to satisfy their sexual and egotistical desires.

Interestingly, as a mother-pastora, Esperanza also subverts the virgin/whore dichotomy. She is a mother who goes out into the world in search of her lost daughter, staying true to her spiritual convictions despite posing as a sex worker. Ironically, she impersonates a sex worker although she has not had intercourse with the clients—nor is she a virgin in the literal sense, because she is a widow and a mother, or in the figurative sense, because she does not stay at home and accept the supposed death of her daughter. This intermediate space that Esperanza inhabits evokes a parallel with the biblical image of Christ. Jesus Christ himself declares, "I am the good shepherd. The good shepherd lays down his life for the sheep."[47] Just as Christ "gives his life for his sheep," Esperanza is a mother-pastora because of her intense belief that Blanca is alive and her incredible willingness to enter dangerous places to find her. When the depravity of those who want to sexually exploit her becomes clear, this parallel with Christ reveals a differential consciousness in Esperanza's search for her daughter and the rupture it causes.

Esperanza's suspicion that her daughter has been kidnapped and sold as a sex slave is a double-edged sword. On the one hand, the kidnapping is a horrible possibility, but on the other, it allows for hope that Blanca may still be alive. Esperanza draws on her spirituality to navigate dangerous spaces in search of her daughter, and it is this spirituality that helps her to survive these experiences. The *limpia* that Esperanza performs in the Pink Palace is an example of using folkloric religiosity as a tool against sexual slavery.[48] Even in a brothel, the prostitutes and the woman in charge, Doña Trini, wish for Esperanza's limpia to rid themselves of bad spirits. Esperanza takes advantage of the limpia to inquire about what Doña Trini is hiding in the "Scarlet Room." Convinced that the room contains young women as prisoners, including Blanca, Esperanza gives a limpia performance to make all of the women believe that they are being purified. The paradox of pureness in a transgressive space like a brothel demonstrates the power of folkloric religious expression. As Laura E. Pérez explains in *Chicana Art: The Politics of Spiritual and Aesthetic Altarities*:

> The "spirit work" of Chicana visual, performing, and literary artists studied here counters the trivialization of the spiritual, particularly of beliefs and practices from non-Western traditions, as "folk religion," "superstitious," or "primitive." It attempts to derail Eurocentric cultural evolutionary arguments in the sphere of religious belief or disbelief that demean that which is culturally different as inferior.[49]

Pérez determines that it is the spirit work of the Chicana novel that challenges the degradation of folklore as an expression of third-world people with primitive religiosities. Through her limpia, Esperanza discovers that, in fact, there are not kidnapped girls in the Scarlet Room but rather Doña Trini's hidden sexual fetish: a cow called Felicitas, the Sixth. This discovery enables Esperanza to continue her search in other spaces and, in this way, fulfill her role as a mother-pastora. Entering transgressive spaces, she finally finds her daughter, ironically, back in her own home. Esperanza represents a spiritual leader because of her astonishing faith incited by apparitions of San Judas Tadeo. Her belief gives her the conviction to directly confront sex trafficking. In the process, the novel offers a message about human trafficking and sex slavery as a result of the neoliberalism embraced by first world countries such as the United States, as well as the detrimental policies enacted by the US government against migrants crossing the border.

Esperanza's literal border crossing is one representation that signifies the leadership of Latin American women to provide a better life for their children. In 2018 the Trump administration's Department of Homeland Security inhumanely separated thousands of children from their parents as they were apprehended by Border Patrol or simply seeking asylum at port entries. According to an article in the *Washington Post* from February 13, 2023, the Department of Homeland Security reports 3,924 children that were separated from their parents "from the day Trump was inaugurated until the day he left office." Of these, 2,926 children have been reunited with their parents, 148 are in the "process of reunification," 183 "informed of opportunity to reunify," and 667 children are "not in process," meaning there is no process for reunification. In other words, 998 children are still not with their parents and were separated from their parents by the state.[50] And, the heart-wrenching endeavors of reuniting the children with their parents has been at the forefront of discussions of violent racism manifesting along the US-Mexico border, and it is this narrative of a mother looking for a child across borders that defines the main plot of *Esperanza's Box of Saints*. After searching for her lost child in dangerous and taboo spaces, she finds and places them in the sacred place: returned to the care and healing of the mother. Spiritual, female headship recentered in Castillo's and Escandón's novels is a relevant conversation of the transnational experience of women of color and their children living through circumstances of racism and sexual violence and their survival of such violence.

Conclusion

Toward the end of the twentieth century and the beginning of the twenty-first, women have become more involved in leadership, even within the Catholic Church.[51] The Chicana cultural production presented in this chapter demonstrates the rising spiritual expression of women practicing leadership roles. These works reveal that the mother does not have the same iconographic meaning as she has in the past within Chicana culture. Yolanda López, the first Chicana artist to depict the Virgen of Guadalupe in nontraditional ways, argues that the holy mother, the Virgen of Guadalupe, is not the only image representing the Chicana woman. Now, the woman is represented as an active mother, ready to show her love for her children. The love of La Madre has the goal of decolonizing her children to achieve social equality. In this way, the Chicana, by being a mother, draws on her leadership to mobilize her community.

This rings true regarding the migratory experience of many young mothers from Central America and Mexico, turning to the option of crossing the US-Mexico border for the survival of their children. Castillo and Escandón approach the topic of border crossing in literal as well as metaphysical and spiritual ways, adding to the discussion of the treatment of those who cross borders the question of what their prior and subsequent circumstances are after border crossing, and finally exalting these women through acts of La Madre. The empowerment of people of color does indeed lie in the decolonial love of La Madre who crosses borders, whether they are patriarchal, racial, gendered, or spiritual, to give her children a dignified existence and remembrance. Border crossing, as Anzaldúa has written, is what mainstream and hegemonic power structures deem the sites that the queer, the "sexually deviant," the poor, the unacceptable human beings commit their grand sins. Writers like Ana Castillo and María Amparo Escandón transform border crossing into the ultimate form of rising above these power structures in ways that are dignifying and brave.

CHAPTER FIVE

THE COATLICUE STATE AND MOEBIUS STRIP

Mirrors and Mirroring in Artwork of the US-Mexico Border

The US-Mexico border wall is a site of division and intimidation, signaling to those who encounter it that they are not welcome. One of President Donald J. Trump's major campaign promises in 2016 was to build a "big, beautiful wall," and he infamously proclaimed, "When Mexico sends its people, they're not sending their best . . . They're sending people that have lots of problems, and they're bringing those problems with us. They're bringing drugs. They're bringing crime. They're rapists. And some, I assume, are good people."[1] The invocation of Mexico and those who migrate from Mexico as criminals and rapists was a clearly racist claim to justify white supremacist ideals such as not allowing migrants of color into the United States to maintain a white majority in its population. The US-Mexico border wall is a signifier of racial exclusion and violence, and it mirrors to those of us who critically gaze upon it the violence that is enacted by the US government against migrants of color. It is this mirroring effect that I will be studying in this chapter through analysis of mirror and mirroring art by Mexican and Chicanx artists.

Mirrors present us with reflections of life but they also create illusions of life as it could be. Used decoratively, they render the illusion of space, multiplying forms and images beyond any logical boundaries. Even more unsettling manifestations of mirroring demand an analysis of our own subjectivity. They compel us to reckon with and recognize who we are. This is the effect of the use of mirrors in art: destabilization, and thus a renewed awareness of reality, a borderlands consciousness of the reality of the effects of the structure that is the border wall. Artists' efforts to destabilize and decolonize through mirroring are at the root of this chapter. Specifically, I look at art addressing the US-Mexico border wall, where mirrors and mirroring force the observer to come to terms with the violence, racism, and colonization being reflected. I analyze Ana Teresa Fernández's performance art *Borrando la Frontera* (Erasing the Border) (2011), the performance piece *Re/flecting the Border* (2017) by Margarita Certeza Garcia and Marcos Ramírez ERRE, and Ronald Rael's installation *Teeter-Totter Wall* (2019). Utilizing mirrors and mirroring, these artists attempt to decolonize notions of space and identity, create the illusion and possibilities of the wall's absence, and expose the various ways in which violence manifests along the US-Mexico borderlands.

Violences of the Border

Johan Galtung theorized that the dynamics of violence can be mapped in the same way one maps the grammar of a sentence in the English language: subject-verb-object. The subject represents the perpetrator of violence, the verb the act of violence, and the object the victim of violence.[2] Galtung's mapping is useful in distinguishing the various ways in which violence manifests along the US-Mexico borderlands: the US government is the subject (the actor that enacts the verb), the verb (the action) is the violence it inflicts, and the objects (the receivers of the action) are communities of color as well as the earth and its resources. I group these violences into four related categories: violence of division, environmental violence, sacrilegious violence, and violence of negligence.

Violence of division refers to the literal and figurative separation imposed upon both migrants and *fronterizos* (people living in borderland communities) by this state boundary. It is well documented that the border wall, a long structure that cuts through the land, has deleterious effects on natural habitats and local wildlife. Although Galtung's definition of violence does not include nonhuman victims, Horacio de la Cueva Salcedo, a researcher in environmental biology at the Centro de Investigación Científica y de Educación Superior de Ensenada in Mexico, defines environmental violence as "the use and extraction of natural resources in such a way as to preclude their sustainable use."[3] This explanation intertwines the welfare of the land, its resources, natural habitats, and animals with that of the humans that inhabit the land. Thus, violences inflicted on the environment—the land and wildlife—will inevitably affect human beings, including future generations that live in that space. Building the border wall has been shown to have such consequences, as flooding along the Texas-Mexico border has led to disrupted migration patterns and the deaths of thousands of plants and animals.

Moreover, as La Cueva Salcedo argues, such environmental devastation impacts human populations in many ways. At the border, this often manifests as sacrilegious violence. In addition to the ongoing theft of Indigenous land—a continuous violence enacted by the settler-colonial states of the United States and Mexico—ravaging natural habitats destroys sacred Indigenous sites and vegetation, such as at the Organ Pipe Cactus National Monument in Arizona. This sacrilegious violence does further psychological damage to Indigenous tribes inhabiting the borderlands.

Finally, violence of negligence has always impacted people at the border but has been especially deadly during the COVID-19 pandemic of 2020 and 2021. Vulnerable border communities, as well as the migrants who cross the border, many consisting of people of color, have had to confront a US government bent on constructing a border wall despite the pandemic, even as out-of-state construction crews exacerbate the spread of the deadly SARS-CoV-2 virus. Such violence of negligence demonstrates a blatant and racialized disregard for human life.

Thus, by building the border wall, the US government has and continues to desecrate Indigenous sacred sites, destroy natural habitats, physically separate people living in sister cities through a militaristic boundary, and wantonly endanger their lives. But although such violences escalated during the Trump presidency, past presidents such as George W. Bush and Barack Obama also built portions of the border wall at the Texas-Mexico boundary. Indeed, on a 2019 tour I took of the Santa Ana National Wildlife Refuge, scholar and activist Stefanie Herweck expressed that the Sierra Club was active in opposing border wall construction during Obama's two terms. She was quick to point out that such activism is nonpartisan; the Sierra Club has had to fight both Democratic and Republican administrations for the environmental well-being of the Rio Grande Valley. As Herweck's statement indicates, state violence at the border is nothing new, even as Trump's policies, active border wall construction, and the COVID-19 pandemic have exacerbated it.

Chicanx Artists Critique the Border

As a case in point, Chicanx artists have been critiquing the violence at the US-Mexico border for decades. Performance artist Guillermo Gómez-Peña, for example, has engaged in these criticisms since the 1970s. In one of his most well-known pieces, *The Border Wedding* (1988), he and fellow performance artist Emily Hicks staged a wedding at the Tijuana–San Diego border wall. Gómez-Peña and Hicks, who was seven months pregnant, stood facing each other on either side of the wall: a powerful symbol of the border's violence in separating loved ones and inevitably affecting future generations. In *Border Brujo*, another 1988 piece, Gómez-Peña adorned himself in "cultural fetish items, and ... a border patrolman's jacket decorated with buttons, bananas, beads, and shells" to sharply critique US violence toward Brown and Black immigrants at the border while simultaneously upholding colonialist attitudes toward Mexican culture.[4]

Chicana artist Consuelo Jiménez Underwood also takes on the border wall in her piece *The Sacred Jump* (1994). Intertwining textiles and wire to construct a type of fencing barrier, Jiménez

Underwood created a tapestry of contemporary and ancient Aztec religious imagery. She depicts Mictlantecuhtli, the Aztec lord of the dead, known as a guide for souls entering Mictlan, the realm of the underworld. His presence at the border wall is significant, as Jiménez Underwood not only portrays the border itself as a violent space but also the way that passage into the United States can be actual hell for migrants, particularly those who are undocumented. As Gary Keller, author of *Contemporary Chicana and Chicano Art: Artists, Works, Culture, and Education,* writes of Jiménez Underwood's representation of Mictlantecuhtli and Mictlan, "This mythological place can be viewed as a modern metaphor for the United States, most notably since it was purported to have been located in the north. The harrowing and dangerous journey made by the dead serves as an allegory for the treacherous travels of the undocumented."[5]

In addition, Jiménez Underwood's piece includes an image that has become a metonym of undocumented life: a "caution" sign with silhouettes of a father, mother, and child running. This "familia crossing" image has been racialized to depict Brown and Black undocumented people in the United States. However, it has also been appropriated by Chicanx artists to criticize the violence enacted toward families at the border, many choosing to cut out the caution portion of the image. Rosa M., a Chicana artist that works with mixed media, ceramics, acrylic paint, stained glass, and carved wood, created a piece in 1994 featuring the familia crossing image. Titled *La Sagrada Familia de Aztlan,* the piece is reminiscent of the carved wooden *altares* that *santeros* built to venerate saints in New Mexico and Mexico. At the top of the altar in Rosa M.'s piece, a cross stands on a sacred heart that has wrapped around the thorn crown of Christ. In its center is the familia crossing image, with "La Sagrada Familia" written above and "En Aztlan 1994" below. Again, we see religious iconography used to signal the sacrilegious violence of the border wall and the state-sponsored violence of division of undocumented people through detention and deportation.

The Coatlicue State and Moebius Strip

More recently, Mexican and Chicanx artists have begun critiquing the violence of the border and the construction of the border wall with mirroring. As an artistic medium, mirroring produces powerful symbolism and, as a theoretical concept, fosters discussions of subjectivity. In Jacques Lacan's formulation, mirrors reflect back to us a version of ourselves in which we are no longer subjective but objective. While we, looking at our reflections, remain in a subjective state of perpetual longing, lacking something that we believe will fulfill us, the reflection itself lacks nothing, needs nothing; it just is. In other words, subjectivity is defined by deficiency and want; objectivity is satisfaction, no longer desiring what is missing. This understanding of mirroring is significant in art installations and performances at the border wall. As a geopolitical division separating two nation-states, mirroring conceptualizes the US-Mexico border as an artificial line in the region's landscape, one that creates longing for an undivided land, yet the reality is environmental violence, violence of division, and violence of neglect. The longing of a landscape that is not cut through with a border wall is a borderlands consciousness, in which border communities imagine a world in which they are not subjected to the US government imposing a forced division with the construction of a border wall and the military apparatus used to enforce immigration laws. Using mirrors and mirroring, Mexican and Chicanx artists have evoked this longing by creating reflections and optical illusions that depict the region as a landscape without borders. Such art highlights not only this subjective longing but also the ability to achieve objectivity in the resulting reflections. Moreover, in erasing the border through mirrors and mirroring, these artists also expose what has been lost through its violences: the communities that lose their land, the landscape that is destroyed, and the wildlife that is killed for the sake of the border wall. In this way, the artists use mirroring as a mode of decolonization.

Likewise, Gloria Anzaldúa's theorization of mirrors and mirroring offers a poignant frame for analyzing border wall art. She writes in *Borderlands / La Frontera: The New Mestiza*:

> There is another quality to the mirror and that is the act of seeing. Seeing and being seen. Subject and object, I and she. The eye pins down the object of its gaze, scrutinizes it, judges it . . . but in a glance also lies awareness, knowledge. These seemingly contradictory aspects—the act of being seen, held immobilized by a glance, and "seeing through" an experience—are symbolized by the underground aspects . . . [which] I call the Coatlicue state.[6]

Coatlicue is an Aztec deity—a statue of whom resides in the National Museum of Anthropology in Mexico City—depicted as a woman with no head but instead two snakes mirroring one another. Representing opposing or clashing identities within one being, she is the essence of Anzaldúa's Coatlicue state: "Coatlicue depicts the contradictory. . . . she is a symbol of the fusion of opposites." To be in the Coatlicue state is to "cross over" from a place of psychological paralysis to a place of knowing; it is attaining knowledge.[7] The US-Mexico border is a physical manifestation of the Coatlicue state. The artwork analyzed here represents overcoming the Coatlicue state in order to cross over and attain the knowledge that the border is a construct, an imposition over the land by settler-colonial nation-states.

This experience of crossing over is indeed a liminal one. In his essay "On the Other Side of the Mexican Mirror," Gómez-Peña articulates this liminality by describing the US-Mexico border as a Moebius strip. A Moebius strip is a mathematical concept that describes a surface that has only one side and one boundary; it is unorientable and represents infinity. Gómez-Peña explains:

> And so, when I crossed the border, I unwittingly started my irreversible process of Pocho-ization or de-Mexicanization. . . . I

found that once you cross the border you could never really go back. Whenever I tried, I always ended up "on the other side," as if walking on a Moebius strip.... Eventually, it was my art and my literature that granted me the full citizenship denied to me by both countries. I invented my own conceptual country. In the "inverted cartography" of my performances and writings, Chicanos and US Latinos became the mainstream culture, with Spanglish as the lingua franca, and mono-cultural Anglos became an ever-shrinking minority (Waspbacks or Waspanos) unable to participate in the public life of "my" country because of their unwillingness to learn Spanish and embrace our culture.[8]

In declaring the US-Mexico border a Moebius strip, Gómez-Peña's artwork is a fluid expression traversing the border. He walks the Moebius strip as he pleases, centering the US-Mexico borderlands as an "inverted cartography"—a regional space that is beautiful, brings life, and resists colonization every day. Moreover, conceptualizing the border as a Moebius strip recognizes the artificiality of the boundary itself; it cleverly comprises not two sides but one. Thus, both Anzaldúa and Gómez-Peña theorize the US-Mexico border experience as one of simultaneous duality and singularity. When Chicanx and Mexican artists employ mirrors and mirroring at the US-Mexico border, they not only critique the border wall itself but also reveal who and what it is hurting.

Mirrors and Mirroring in Border Wall Art

The Trump presidency (2016–2020), while building on earlier efforts to both physically and culturally reinforce the US-Mexico border, undoubtedly heightened the violences cast against migrants, fronterizos, and the environments that constitute the US-Mexico borderlands. Trump's anti-immigrant policy and rhetoric, response to the COVID-19 pandemic, and extensive border wall construction have had far-reaching consequences. Artists' use of mirrors and mirroring in their work show to the world these consequences, decolonizing the border by imagining its erasure and exposing its brutality in various ways.

Ana Teresa Fernández, a Mexican-born multimedia artist based in San Francisco, uses mirroring to expose the artificiality of the border wall in her 2011 piece *Borrando la Frontera*. Fernández painted a portion of the wall itself with Behr P500-2 Seashore Dreams, transforming rust-colored steel into a blue that mimics the ocean and sky beyond it. The effect is one of erasure, an optical illusion producing a "hole" in the wall. As Matthew Harrison Tedford writes in an article for *Sculpture Nature*, "*Borrando la Frontera* is a simple but abrupt challenge to any acquired normalcy. The erasure begs the question, 'What if this were all gone?'"[9] Indeed, Fernández's use of mirroring to create the illusion of a hole in the border wall evokes longing for a landscape that was once untouched, unbordered, free. This notion of a borderless Tijuana–San Diego beach represents the overcoming of the Coatlicue state, where there is no longer a clash between nation-states but rather a continuous, uninterrupted landscape.

In erasing the border wall, even if only by illusion, Fernández's *Borrando la Frontera* disrupts US governmental efforts of brutal divisiveness and racialized violence toward those who inhabit the borderlands. Regarding her choice to paint on the Tijuana side of the wall, she explains, "I do it on the Mexican side because that wall exists for Mexicans. In San Diego, there's lots of beaches, but in Tijuana, that's the only beach people congregate at. I'm doing it for the Mexicans who go there on their day off to rest and meditate and exercise, and they're met with this visual obstruction."[10] Fernández's *Borrando la Frontera* imagines a borderlands in which a border wall does not exist, allowing local communities to flourish undisturbed by military warfare and environmental destruction.

Indeed, the erasure created by mirrors in *Borrando la Frontera* invites the question of what the borderlands might look like if there was no border. The answer to this question resides in absence—in

Figure 1. Ana Teresa Fernandez, BORRANDO LA FRONTERA, 2011. Courtesy of the artist and Catharine Clark Gallery.

exposing how the border wall affects the flora, fauna, and people that inhabit these regions, as well as what has already been lost. Despite the Trump administration's attempts to prove that border wall construction does not inflict damage on the natural world, there is much evidence to the contrary. The Santa Ana National Wildlife Refuge located in Hidalgo, Texas, for example, is a 2,088-acre landscape along the Rio Grande. It was established in 1943 to protect migratory birds because it is "positioned along an east-west and north-south juncture of two major migratory routes for many species of birds".[11] Because the area is vulnerable to flooding from the nearby Rio Grande, the refuge is surrounded by tall cement levees, about thirteen to fifteen feet high.

When Congress approved $1.3 billion to construct a border

wall, "including the addition of 33 miles of steel-bollard fencing" through neighboring counties, "the measure prohibited that money from being used to build through Santa Ana."[12] According to Scott Nicol, chair of the Sierra Club's Borderlands Campaign, the Trump administration "split hairs" to claim adherence to the mandate without truly maintaining the protections put in place to safeguard the reserve.[13] As part of border wall construction, steel bollard fencing was placed on top of the Santa Ana levees, leading to flooding and the deaths of hundreds of animals. Nicol explained the problem on a local television station:

> That is because the 6-inch-wide steel bollards, to be spaced 4 inches apart, could clog with debris in heavy rains, and cause flooding of homes and lands in this flood-prone region, especially in Starr County, he said. "An animal that is small enough to squeeze through a four-inch gap pretty much could, but nothing else will. Ocelots will never fit through that. Bobcats and lots of the species that move around through the wildlife refuges can't squeeze through a 4-inch gap."[14]

These environmental catastrophes come to mind in the analysis of Fernández's performance art erasing the border, as it allows the imagination to conceptualize a reality in which the wildlife of the US-Mexico borderlands is not killed by steel bollard fencing. Erasing the border created a portal into this reality in which environmental violence by a border wall is nonexistent: it is a Moebius strip, as Gómez-Peña articulates, in which both sides of the border are actually the same side. The border wall is directly responsible for environmental violence along the US-Mexico borderlands.

Tragically, environmental violence is not limited to the Santa Ana National Wildlife Refuge or the Texas border region. In April 2019, the Center for Biological Diversity, a nonprofit organization that seeks to protect endangered wildlife through scientific data and legal action, issued a statement admonishing the Trump administration for plans to build an eighty-mile bollard-style wall along the Arizona and New Mexico border. Arguing that the border wall would endanger the wildlife of the region, the statement read:

> The New Mexico wall will cut through the remote Chihuahuan Desert and sever a known migratory corridor for Mexican gray wolves, among the rarest mammals on the continent. The New Mexico area is also home to the endangered Aplomado falcon, as well as kit foxes, bighorn sheep and ringtails. The Yuma wall will block people and wildlife from accessing the Lower Colorado River. It will also harm habitat for endangered birds including yellow-billed cuckoos, southwestern willow flycatchers and Yuma clapper rails.[15]

Although there are safeguards and laws in place to protect the landscape and wildlife, the statement also revealed that in building the wall the Trump administration waived "more than 30 environmental and cultural laws, including one that dictates how Native American remains are treated."[16]

As this statement indicates, environmental and sacrilegious violence go hand in hand, as such blatant disregard for environmental regulations also violates laws protecting lands that Indigenous people consider sacred. The Trump administration brough about mass destruction of saguaro plants by using dynamite blasts and bulldozers to destroy saguaro plants in preparation for construction at planned border wall sites. The saguaro plant is an invaluable part of the ecosystem of the Sonoran Desert and sacred to the Tohono O'odham tribe. According to the US Department of Agriculture:

> The saguaro is a keystone species that provides food and shelter for many desert animals. Saguaros have hundreds of flowers that bloom several [times] per day from late April to early June. The flowers open at night and close the following afternoon. Lesser long-nosed bats visit the flowers at night. Birds, mostly white-winged doves, and insects, mostly honeybees, visit the flowers the following morning. The fruits mature in June and

early July. The rind splits into three or four sections that peel back to expose the juicy red pulp embedded with up to 2,000 tiny seeds. The fruits ripen during the peak of drought in the early summer and are about the only moist food source for many birds, mammals, and insects during this part of the year. Saguaros make excellent nesting places for many birds.[17]

It is thus with good reason that the United Nations designated Organ Pipe Cactus National Monument—"a pristine example of an intact Sonoran Desert ecosystem" and home to thousands of saguaro plants—as an international biosphere reserve. The environmental violence inflicted on the Sonoran Desert's ecosystem in destroying this plant to build the border wall is deeply troubling. Moreover, the Tohono O'odham tribe's spiritual connection to the land and the saguaro plant in particular is a compounding sacrilegious violence that is truly obscene. Of the saguaro, Tohono O'odham tribal chair Ned Norris Jr. expressed in an interview, "They're our ancestors. They're our remnants of who we are as a people, throughout this whole area. And it's our obligation, it's our duty to do what is necessary to protect that."[18]

The sacred saguaro being blasted and uprooted, fatal flooding in the Santa Ana Wildlife Reserve, and interrupted migration routes for rare and endangered animals are just a few examples of the effects of the border wall on regional landscapes and Indigenous communities. Artwork that uses mirrors and mirroring to imagine the erasure of the US-Mexico border, such as Fernández's *Borrando la Frontera*, exposes the pain and loss of the environmental and sacrilegious violence created by this artificial boundary because it brings about a borderlands consciousness that envisions a borderlands without a border wall. The imagining of a borderlands that is free of a dividing structure cutting through the landscape, as Anzaldúa writes, created an "open wound," an untouched sacred space in which the flora, fauna, and wildlife are respected and loved. By using paint to erase the border wall, Fernández's mirror art brings about a borderlands consciousness.

Violence of Division and Neglect along the US-Mexico Borderlands

Unfortunately, recent construction of the border wall has exacerbated further violence in more ways than with environmental violence. In some cases, it is the physical boundary of the wall itself that upsets local economies. The Department of Homeland Security (DHS) under the Trump administration used eminent domain litigation to waive laws protecting private property owners in service of border wall construction. For example, the DHS has been pressuring Texas landowner José Alfredo Cavazos (also known as Fred Cavazos) to sign a right of entry agreement to build a portion of the wall through his property. Cavazos owns seventy-seven acres of land alongside the Rio Grande—the legal boundary between the nations as designated by the Treaty of Guadalupe Hidalgo—and requires access to the river to raise cattle and maintain his recreational fishing business.[19] As a seventy-year-old man whose mobility depends on a motorized wheelchair, this is his only sources of income. Cavazos and his cousin Reynaldo (Rey) Anzaldúa have been vocal in their efforts to resist the DHS, declaring, "If this goes through, our property's useless."[20]

Cavazos is not alone in fighting the DHS's efforts to forcefully take his land to build the wall. According to a February 2020 NPR broadcast out of Austin, "So far, 55 property owners have gone to court to try to block the survey and construction crews." Jeremy Barnard, owner of the River Bend Resort and Golf Club in Brownsville, Texas, for example, fought the DHS in court in an attempt to retain land. Barnard, a loyal Trump supporter, explained that since much of the border wall would be built on existing levees that extend through the resort property, the wall would kill the business. Many of the other property owners have agricultural businesses growing crops like onions, cotton, and corn—enterprises that would also have difficulty surviving a thirty-foot wall in their midst.[21]

Moreover, while Trump's DHS tried to force landowners to sell portions of their property to build the border wall, active construction of the wall during the COVID-19 pandemic has exacerbated the spread of the virus along the US-Mexico borderlands: this was violence of neglect. Since February 2020, when COVID-19 began to rage throughout the United States, there have been multiple reports of construction crews being transported to the region to build. For example, the Trump administration sent crews to the border in Nogales, Arizona, in April 2020, despite the fact that the state's COVID-19 infection rates were starting to climb. According to Gail Emrick, executive director of the Southeast Arizona Area Health Education Center, "They are bringing people as far away as places like Nebraska and Montana. . . . It's just bringing an irrational level of danger to these communities."[22] Arizona congressman Raúl Grijalva also spoke about border wall construction crews in Ajo, Arizona: "As the rest of the country shuts down to stop the spread of COVID-19, construction crews continue building Trump's vanity wall with billions of dollars in stolen funds. . . . The presence of large construction crews in small border towns threatens the health of those communities where they are already underprepared to deal with the coming 'public health emergency.'"[23] Likewise, Esequiel Salas, mayor of Columbus, New Mexico, expressed concern about the arrival of construction crews and even sent a letter to the company overseeing the project to ask them to delay the work.[24] In June 2020, the *Los Angeles Times* also reported that there were no COVID-19 precautions accompanying wall construction in the Texas Rio Grande Valley: "Nayda Alvarez said she has caught border wall surveyors—without masks or other protective gear—sneaking onto her property along the Rio Grande several times this year, most recently in April."[25] Bringing construction crews to the region during the pandemic clearly puts local communities in danger and constitutes violence of neglect: during a global pandemic with an extremely contagious virus that causes severe illness, the US government put the community in harm's way by bringing in outside crews and exposing the community to the virus.

Moreover, many of these border communities include large numbers of groups that are particularly vulnerable to serious complications from COVID-19. As of 2018, people over age sixty-two account for 34.2 percent of Nogales's population, and in Ajo approximately 41.2 percent of the population is over age sixty.[26] Additionally, there is growing evidence of racial disparities in the severity and spread of COVID-19, affecting Latino and Black communities much more than white communities. In July 2020, the *New York Times* found that the infection rate for African Americans and Latinos was three times higher than whites.[27] Nogales's population is 94.8 percent Latino and Ajo's is 41 percent Latino.[28] The ongoing presence of outside construction crews, there to build a wall that the community does not want during a global pandemic that disproportionately affects their health, is violent.

Such violence of neglect is rooted in racist and xenophobic arguments about COVID-19 used to justify wall construction. When initial reports of the virus were released in February 2020, Trump's order to close the border quickly morphed into blaming immigrants for bringing COVID-19 into the United States. In an April 2020 *Guardian* article, reporter Samuel Gilbert wrote:

> Throughout the Covid-19 crisis, Trump has rationalized border wall construction as a way to contain the spread of the disease. "The Democrat policy of open borders is a direct threat to the health and wellbeing of all Americans," [Trump] said at a rally in South Carolina. "Now, you see it with the coronavirus."
> Public health experts say these claims have little basis, because the virus is not spreading into the US from Mexico—it is already spreading within US communities."[29]

Accusing migrants of color of bringing disease into the United States is not new, as was discussed in chapter 2 of this book regarding the use of Zyklon B and other chemicals on migrants in the early twentieth century. It is a violence of division: the government is sending out the message that migrants (mostly of color) are bringing disease, leading to dangerous policies such as Remain in Mexico and Title 42, a public health order brought into place due to the COVID-19

Figure 2. Ronald Rael, TEETER-TOTTER WALL, *2019. Courtesy of the artist.*

pandemic by the US Center for Disease Control and Prevention (CDC) in 2020. Title 42 is from the Public Health Service Act of 1944, which gave the US surgeon general the power to bar "introduction, transmission, or spread of communicable diseases from foreign countries into the States"; this authority was transferred to the CDC in 1966.[30] President Trump ordered that Title 42 be activated in 2020 despite scientists at the CDC indicating that "there was no evidence that it would slow the virus's spread in the U.S.," and Dr. Anthony Fauci, the leading expert in infectious disease, stated that migrants were not increasing cases of COVID-19.[31] As I type this chapter in 2022, Title 42 is still activated. The dehumanization of migrants as carriers of disease has led to the violence of division: an othering of migrants as diseased and therefore their treatment as a national threat.

Decolonizing the Border: Affirming Community through Mirroring

The violence of division is also at the center of the borderlands consciousness evoked by the mirror artwork titled *Re/flecting the Border* by Margarita Certeza Garcia and Marcos Ramírez ERRE in February 2017. They challenge the imposed violence of division by asserting that communities cannot be divided by an arbitrary state boundary. On February 26, 2017, on the same Tijuana–San Diego beach as Fernández's piece, the artists placed tall mirrors up against the steel border wall next to a sixteen-by-four-foot table. The reflected table, set for dinner, created an optical illusion, again, of a hole in the border—a portal through which communities separated by this barrier can be united once again. The effect echoes Gómez-Peña's Moebius strip, the dinner party across the border suggesting that people of the borderlands maintain community despite the border's presence and its violences. Additionally, Garcia and ERRE's installation gives border communities command of the landscape; it is a borderlands consciousness in which the mirrors erase the line dividing the region and expose it as a one-sided strip on which fronterizos walk.

This experience is somewhat a reality in Friendship Park—a binational park located in the Tijuana–San Diego border region. At Friendship Park, families and friends from both sides of the border are able to gather, despite a fence separating them. Each April, on Día de los Niños (Children's Day), state agents permit a door to be opened and families can physically reunite, hug, and spend the day together. Tragically, this allowance has been rescinded during the COVID-19 pandemic. Even so, mirror art like García and ERRE's challenges such violence of separation and demonstrates border communities' determination to recreate a Día de los Niños at the will of the people, not the state. *Re/flecting the Border* demands that the observer look at the border community members' longing to have fellowship with their kin that live on the other side of the border. It brings the border community into a border consciousness that embraces the Coatlicue state: "Seeing and being seen. Subject and object, I and she. The eye pins down the object of its gaze, scrutinizes it, judges it ... but in a glance also lies awareness, knowledge," as this seeing allows the dream of one day sharing a meal with loved ones despite the border that separates them. The Coatlicue state is the knowledge that resistance to policies and legislation that further divides the border community will lead to what *Re/flecting the Border* visually represents: a table full of loved ones that runs right through the US-Mexico border wall.

Likewise, Ronald Rael's *Teeter-Totter Wall*—a 2019 installation of bright pink seesaws, or teeter-totters, straddling the border wall in Sunland Park, New Mexico, and Ciudad Juárez—exhibits both the violence of the border and the bonds it cannot break. Inspired by his own drawings—published in his book *Borderwall as Architecture: A Manifesto for the US-Mexico Boundary*—in response to the Secure Fence Act of 2006, Rael recorded videos of people riding the seesaws and posted them to his Instagram account. His caption read, "The wall became a literal fulcrum for US-Mexico relations and children and adults were connected in meaningful ways on both sides with the recognition that the actions that take place on one side have a direct consequence on the other side."[32] Rael explained in an interview that as he and a group of helpers were installing the seesaws, both US Border Patrol agents and Mexican soldiers arrived on their respective sides of the wall to question what they were doing. They allowed the group to continue the project, and Rael invited the state agents to participate in the play. He mused, "Wouldn't it be great if we could have gotten a Border Patrol agent and a [Mexican] soldier to ride the teeter-totter together?"[33] The possibility of two agents of their respective nation-states, whose purpose is violence, coming together and playing on the teeter-totter demonstrates the power of child's play as a way of humanizing the Other and bringing that borderlands consciousness to the community as well as to their oppressors.

The seesaw is also a representation of the effects of the violence on both sides of the border because despite the ability to play

Figure 3. Ronald Rael, TEETER-TOTTER WALL, *2019. Courtesy of the artist.*

with someone on the other side of the wall, you are still separated from them. This separation is a very real experience: the detention of families fleeing Central America, the separation of children from their parents, the femicides in Mexico (referenced in the teeter-totters' pink hue), and the August 2019 mass shooting at an El Paso Walmart in which the gunman declared in a manifesto his intention to kill Mexicans. At the same time, the use of a children's toy to portray the interconnectedness of the border region and the fronterizo community is stark, impactful, and beautiful to watch. The Moebius strip effect of the seesaw play in the videos is palpable: the border wall is there, but human relationships shatter it. Such mirror art reveals that the wall cannot truly separate the US-Mexico borderlands or its people, regardless of how high, big, or "beautiful" it is. The fronterizo community transcends the border; it will never quash the fire of la gente that has survived centuries of colonialism and violence.

By waving laws that protect the environment, property rights, and religious freedom, spending billions of dollars on building the border wall, justifying it in the name of national security, and neglecting public health in the midst of a pandemic, the US government is violently acting upon the communities and wildlife of the US-Mexico borderlands. Chicanx and Mexican artists like Ana Teresa Fernández, Margarita Certeza Garcia and Marcos Ramírez ERRE, and Ronald Rael expose and condemn this violence through their art. Using mirrors and mirroring to create the illusion of erasure, they demonstrate that while the damage is very real, the border is not. Like a Moebius strip, there is no boundary there: only communities and land that cannot be disconnected by an arbitrary state line.

CHAPTER SIX

MAKING WAVES IN "TRANQUIL WATERS"

Chicanafuturism and the Invisibilization of Violence

As with everything since March 2020, the COVID-19 global pandemic has severely disrupted supply chains across the world, impacting goods from food to medical equipment. As I write this chapter, there is a baby formula shortage that has parents reeling as grocery store shelves are empty and their babies go hungry. The roots of these shortages are multifaceted, with experts pointing to three major factors: workforce disruptions as people get sick with the virus, monopolization within industries (as with the baby formula shortage of 2022), and bottlenecking along the supply chain as each link struggles to keep up with demand.[1] However, another significant issue is worker mistreatment. In the last year, unionization has increased across industries in response to poor working conditions during the COVID-19 pandemic, including in major corporations like Amazon and Starbucks. Workers' protests and unionization have led to considerable changes in the way these corporations do business.

Even so, the pandemic has also facilitated the rise of maquiladoras—companies that expedite the production of goods in factories that are mostly duty- and tariff-free—especially in cities south of the US-Mexico border like Tijuana and Mexicali. In December 2021, the *San Francisco Chronicle* reported on the mistreatment of workers in medical maquiladoras. Predominantly impoverished women of color living in "migrant worker communities," these workers assembled vital equipment for managing COVID-19, such as "ventilators, respirators, masks, hospital beds, and more."[2] Mexico is the leading exporter of medical supplies to the United States, yet none of these provisions were intended for use in Mexico during the pandemic.[3]

Moreover, the Trump administration pressured Mexico to keep all medical supply maquiladoras open in 2020, even as most businesses closed due to the surge in infections. Workers, many of whom were members of populations vulnerable to severe COVID-19, were made to work twelve-hour shifts and, if they showed symptoms, were given Ibuprofen instead of being sent home. When maquiladoras were mandated to send workers home with full pay, they gave them only half their wages. But despite this harmful "discrimination and harassment in the workplace," the *Chronicle*'s report failed to make waves amid the supply chain woes dominating the news cycle.[4]

It is this invisibilization of violence toward marginalized communities along the US-Mexico borderlands that frames this chapter. My discussion focuses on an analysis of three pieces of cultural production within the genre of Chicanafuturism: Alejandro Morales's novel *The Rag Doll Plagues* (1991), Alex Rivera's film *Sleep Dealer* (2008), and Rosaura Sánchez and Beatrice Pita's novel *Lunar Braceros, 2125–2148* (2009). These works of speculative fiction depict worlds in the past, present, or future that can be similar to or radically different from our own. In these worlds, invisibilized violence manifests as ecological devastation, the exploitation of racialized communities, new technologies used for violence, and the extraction of human resources resulting in disease and death. But the texts shatter this opacity and expose the violence, as if giving the audience an antidote that enables them to see that which was invisibilized—both within the fictional narratives and the real world. By making invisibilized violence visible, these works of Chicanafuturism convey a borderlands consciousness that reverberates as a force of resistance well beyond the texts themselves.

The Tranquil Waters of Neoliberalism

Neoliberalism emerges as one of the main targets of criticism in these pieces of Chicanafuturist cultural production. Neoliberalism is an economic system in which corporations enjoy an unfettered, unrestrained, and unregulated pursuit of profit, typically at the expense of marginalized communities such as those along the US-Mexico borderlands. When embraced as the global standard, the propensity for exploitation, discrimination, and abuse is very high, as evident in the maquiladora example above.

Neoliberalism evolved from classical liberalism, which Manfred Steger and Ravi K. Roy explain as the prioritization of the ideal of individual freedoms and limiting government action that could infringe on these freedoms. Prior to the twentieth century, the government's role was to "[secure] and [protect] these individual rights, especially property rights."[5] However, the Great Depression forced economists to reevaluate the efficacy of classical liberalism and consider policies to regulate the market and create jobs. Consequently, the United States embarked upon what Steger and Roy call the "Golden Age of Controlled Capitalism" from 1945 to 1975. As they explain, "National governments controlled money flows in and out of their territories. High taxation on wealthy individuals and profitable corporations led to the expansion of the welfare state. Rising wages and increased social services in the wealthy countries of the global North offered workers entry into the middle class."[6] But by the 1970s, inflation was out of control, oil prices quadrupled, and unemployment was on the rise. Economists turned to neoliberalism, arguing that government oversight inhibited economic growth and high tariffs led to inflation.[7] Since the 1980s, governments have established a "global neoliberal development agenda" to foster international free-trade agreements, which after the North American Free Trade Agreement (NAFTA) in 1994 came to accelerate the maquiladora industry in border cities.

According to Steger and Roy, neoliberalism has three dimensions—ideology, mode of governance, and policy. In the United States, these elements have come to define the way the nation functions. Since neoliberalism "puts the production and exchange of material goods at the heart of the human experience," the United States places utmost value on making and owning things.[8] Striving to be a strong competitor in the global free market, the government enacts policies rooted in neoliberal ideology that harm marginalized communities. The US-Mexico borderlands have experienced this violence for decades with the rise of the maquiladora industry starting in the 1970s, the North American Free Trade Agreement (NAFTA) signed in 1992, and other policies that have fostered their impoverishment, impairment, and overall detriment. This violence is as imperceptible as the air we breathe; it is, in Johan Galtung's words, the "tranquil waters" of structural violence.

The sinister nature of structural violence lies in its imperceptibility, its normalization, even as it torments entire groups of people. As Galtung explains, "Structural violence is silent, it does not show—it is essentially static, it *is* the tranquil waters. In a *static* society, personal violence will be registered, whereas structural violence may be seen as about as natural as the air around us. . . . Personal violence may more easily be noticed, even though the 'tranquil waters' of structural violence may contain much more violence."[9] This is true of the violence impacting US-Mexico borderlands communities, such as the invisibilization of Brown and Black laborers, of the militarization of the border, of the development of technology targeting migrants, and of their continued detention in private centers funded by the US government. Maintaining the "tranquil waters" of this invisibilized violence is deliberate; it is a significant means of preserving the status quo. Chicanafuturism analyzed here seeks to stir up these waters, to expose both the violence itself and its invisibilization, and to rouse in the reader a borderlands consciousness.

Chicanafuturism: Making Waves in the Tranquil Waters

As a genre, speculative fiction presents dystopian, utopian, and otherwise alternate realities that resemble our world just enough to be recognizable but remain foreign enough to unsettle the audience's perception of reality, inspire them to examine it, and ultimately enable them to reach a new consciousness. Chicanafuturism as a subgenre manifests itself as speculative fiction in particular ways. Catherine S. Ramírez defines it as "Chicano cultural production that attends to cultural transformations resulting from new and everyday technologies (including their detritus); that excavates, creates, and alters narratives of identity, technology, and the future; that interrogates the promises of science and technology; and that redefines humanism and the human."[10] Further explaining Chicanafuturism's distinctiveness, B. V. Olguín argues that it "[resists] the nihilist impulse of most postmodernist narratives"—that is, there is a borderlands consciousness within Chicanafuturist narratives that pushes us to challenge the violence of unfettered capitalism.[11]

In particular, the borderlands consciousness within these narratives reflects Darko Suvin's concept of "cognitive estrangement." Andrew Uzendoski employs Suvin's formulation in his analysis of Latinx speculative fiction, describing a defamiliarizing process of "reimagining common concepts and objects as uncommon, making the known seem alien."[12] Using cognitive estrangement to bring about a borderlands consciousness is important, as it invites audiences to see things from an alternative perspective. The premise of science fiction is to create a reality within the narrative that is so different from our reality that it sparks an analysis of the problems within our world. But when those problems are representations of real-world issues, that is when a borderlands consciousness springs forth. Uzendoski explains, "Juxtaposing multiple worldviews, cognitive estrangement serves as the mechanism in speculative fiction that spurs the reader to interrogate the dominance of existing social and political systems."[13] That interrogation is borderlands consciousness.

The three Chicanafuturism texts examined in this chapter present speculative fiction regarding the US-Mexico borderlands specifically. They thus emphasize structural and somatic violence produced by government and corporate hegemonies. Enacted through narrative elements like bracero labor on the moon, laborers who are cyborgs linked with robots north of the border, and blood transfusions from Mexicans to cure a deadly disease, the violence depicted in the texts constitutes a cognitive estrangement. Although it does not truly reflect reality, the characters, dialogue, and problems facilitate a borderlands consciousness that evokes real-life issues facing the US-Mexico borderlands today. In particular, the texts engage themes of ecological devastation, the exploitation of racialized peoples, technologies targeting migrants, and the extraction of human resources causing disease and death. In doing so, filmmaker Alex Rivera and novelists Alejandro Morales, Rosaura Sánchez, and Beatrice Pita offer "a rhetoric of change by always questioning the cultural moment . . . attuning [their] readership to the intersections of scientific theory, technological development, and social conventions."[14]

Ecological Devastation

In her analysis of transborder Chicanafuturism, Lysa Rivera argues that such texts "not only offer critical visions of globalization both today and in the near future but also insist on reading late capitalism as a troubling and enduring extension of colonial relations of power between the United States and Mexico."[15] Indeed, colonialism looms large in Chicanafuturism as the origin of violences past, present, and future. Neoliberalism itself has roots in colonialism, as those who sought to conquer other lands did so in the name of individual freedom and capitalistic gain. Likewise, the texts analyzed here portray ecological devastation as a result of colonialism, plundering both the earth and its inhabitants. María Herrera-Sobek explains this dual formulation as environmental ecology and social ecology, each with the potential for destruction and repair.[16] That is, when the social ecology is such that there is equity for all members of a society in access to needs and services such as housing, water and food, waste disposal, and when those basic needs are met, catastrophes like an epidemic would be addressed more adequately as there is not a compounding of morbidity and mortality in the population.

Alejandro Morales begins *The Rag Doll Plagues* by exploring ecological devastation in a speculative version of the colonial past. The novel is split into three parts, each featuring a protagonist physician who must confront a mysterious plague in different times and places: these protagonists are descendants of the first book's protagonist, Gregorio Revueltas. In book 1, Morales alludes to the sixteenth-century conquest in Mexico and subsequent disease, death, and colonialism with the story of a fictitious illness in eighteenth-century Mexico City. Here, Gregorio is sent to Mexico City by the Spanish Crown in 1788. He is to be the new director of the Protomedicato, whose role is to "assess the medical needs of His Majesty's colonies," which extend to helping eradicate a deadly infectious disease called La Mona, which has become an epidemic.[17] Morales writes, "It begins like a pox, but only on the extremities of the body. Then in a few days, it does horrendous damage to the internals. The suffering is great then, but when it gets to the trunk and head, it is indescribable."[18] La Mona leaves the body looking like a rag doll, as evident in the description of a dead girl who has succumbed to the disease: "Her arms and legs were like stockings of skin, grotesquely swollen, reddish blood as is sausage."[19]

Gregorio describes Mexico City as a river filled with death, the stench of human waste and the decaying bodies of humans and animals permeating the air. In a moment of insight, Gregorio thinks to himself, "I finally believed what I was seeing. This was not a nightmare, but His Majesty's Empire."[20] Without explicitly naming colonialism as the culprit of the devastation facing Mexico, Morales makes it clear that the colonial system is a violent one that brings forth filth, disease, and death. Herrera-Sobek describes the "two linkages" created here: "one between ecological issues of human waste, filth, garbage, and improper hygiene and issues of racial and political oppression." She argues, "When both environmental ecology and social ecology are addressed and action is taken to alleviate the stress on the population exerted by these two forces, a healthier climate, both medically and politically speaking, is produced."[21]

In *The Rag Doll Plagues*, it takes four years of devastation to finally reach the healthier climate about which Herrera-Sobek speaks. This is not because Gregorio is ignorant of such ideas about respecting and managing the region's environmental and social ecology. In fact, he is presented with the key for ending the epidemic much earlier, in a conversation with Father Juan Antonio Llorente, general secretary of the Holy Office. This character, known as Father Antonio, has tremendous influence in Mexico City. He is a priest, doctor, historian, and confessor for other powerful people in the city. Also, he is an outspoken critic of the church. When Gregorio asks Father Antonio for advice about treating La Mona as well as better overall conditions in New Spain, Father Antonio lets him have it. Addressing Gregorio as a representative of the Spanish crown, he retorts:

> Simply stop ravaging the resources of Mexico. Leave monies here and designate an appropriate amount of funds for medical services and training. Let the Viceroy know, let the King beware of the possible decimation of the population. The Indian masses reproduce at an alarming rate, but even today they are still the vulnerable to disease. This plague will kill at least a million savages. The Holy Office must stop persecuting the *curanderos* [native healers], for they are an asset to us. Many are truly learned *texoxotla ticitl*, doctors and surgeons.[22]

In effect, Father Antonio is telling Gregorio, head of the king's Protomedicato, that the colonial system of extracting resources from Mexico and lack of care for its Indigenous peoples will ultimately decimate this part of the Spanish empire.

Father Jude, Gregorio's guide, also implicates the colonial regime, making sure to point out, "This disease does not exclusively kill Indians. . . . You and your kind are not immune."[23] This is not merely a warning to preserve Gregorio's safety. By differentiating between La Mona and other diseases brought from Europe, Father Jude clearly suggests that Mexico's environmental ecology, ravaged by colonialism, has everything to do with social ecology—that is, the horrendous conditions Indigenous people have endured under a racist caste system put in place to keep the Spanish in power for centuries. La Mona represents the invisibilization of this violence, as Gregorio could have easily overlooked the underlying problem of a social ecology born and bred on violence against Indigenous people in his quest to find a cure. This invisibilization continues to this day with racism leading many in the medical establishment to refuse to consider social determinants of health that impact racialized populations, including higher rates of disease and death.[24]

In his dialogue with Gregorio, Father Antonio also chastises the Holy Office for subjugating Indigenous curanderos and praises the traditional medicine of the region. Here too he condemns the ecological devastation wrought by colonialism, reflecting the ongoing repression and denigration of native cultures. This was the case with Don Pedrito Jaramillo, a faith healer in Falfurrias, Texas, who treated people on both sides of the border at the beginning of the twentieth century. According to Jennifer Koshatka Seman, during this period the Western medical establishment promoted the idea of "tropical medicine, which combined pseudo-scientific ideas about race with new scientific advances in parasitology, bacteriology, and epidemiology, in efforts to contain and eradicate diseases associated with hot and humid climates."[25] This theory postulated that "foreign" persons of color, such as Mexicans, carried such tropical diseases. This racist pseudoscientific ideology permeated the doctor's office, who because of this ideology discriminated against Mexicans and Mexican Americans. To avoid this discrimination, they sought medical care with Don Pedrito, who not only treated their ailments with traditional medicine but also embraced their cultural identity. Don Pedrito's impact on the Mexican American transborder community was vast; he received up to two hundred letters a week, ranging from expressions of gratitude to requests for *recetas*, recipes for healing.[26]

However, in sharp contrast to the neoliberal fixation with turning a profit, Don Pedrito did not charge for his assistance. And because the local Mexican American community sought him out rather than medical doctors, Don Pedrito's curandero services began to impact the earning potential of area physicians. Consequently, the American Medical Association and US Post Office investigated Don Pedrito for fraud but, ironically, because he never charged any money for his services, the charges were dropped.[27] Just as the European colonial regime viewed people of color practicing traditional medicine as a threat because the purpose of colonialism is to separate colonial subjects from their culture and history, US neoliberalism continued to demonize it well into the twentieth century for interfering with the business of healthcare. By having the character of Father Antonio acknowledge this demonization and its colonialist roots, Morales makes this invisibilized violence against cultural identity visible to his audience.

Along with such efforts to unsettle borderlands communities' cultural identities, attempts to literally close the US-Mexico border are a very real possibility. This already happened when the Trump administration used the COVID-19 pandemic as a justification to close the border from March 2020 to October 2020, exacerbating the struggles of an already stressed immigration legal system and leaving many asylum seekers in Mexico under very dangerous conditions. While this was a temporary closure due to the pandemic, Alex Rivera's 2008 film *Sleep Dealer* presents a fictional world in which the US-Mexico border is closed permanently. In the film, US corporation Del Rio Water has built a dam near a small community in Oaxaca, Mexico, called Santa Ana Del Rio, where the protagonist Memo resides with his family. The dam has blocked local water access and is sending water north to the United States. In order to sustain the scant crops on which Memo's family subsists on their impoverished farm, they must purchase water from Del Rio Water in small bags. To prevent unauthorized access, the corporation has installed a barbed wire fence and security cameras, and has a gun pointed at anyone who approaches the property.

This privatization of water is a violent move toward ecological disaster, as water, a natural resource, is absolutely necessary for life; the presence of water and the way it moves (or is moved) directly affects entire communities. As Adriana Johnson argues, infrastructure like the dam in *Sleep Dealer* is meant to be invisible and to thus invisibilize such violence. She writes, "Insofar as infrastructures serve a specified array of connectivity, they are perceived largely in terms of this functionality. As such, more often than not they are meant to fade into the background as they serve to convey something else: cars, water, electricity. To work properly as infrastructure is to become the unseen ligaments of a world arranged."[28] The violence of the dam near Santa Ana Del Rio is that of limiting the local community's water supply but its functionality as infrastructure invisibilizes the perpetrator: a faceless corporation with extreme wealth and power on both sides of the border and the neoliberal policies that permit the dam's construction in the first place. North of the border, those who benefit from Del Rio Water's dam are oblivious to the violence brought about by their water consumption. In fact, the film depicts a celebration in the corporation's violent practices defending their dam with a fictional reality show featuring live drones attacking people who Del Rio Water claims are threatening their dams.

By exposing both this invisibilized violence and widespread ignorance of it, Rivera's representation leads the audience to consider who has access to water along the US-Mexico borderlands—an issue that remains pertinent. For example, a 1944 treaty between Mexico and the United States stipulates that "every year, Mexico pipes about 114 billion gallons of water north from the Rio Grande and Conchas rivers; the United States sends almost 489 billion gallons south from the Colorado River."[29] Mexico did not comply with the requirement for many years and so began repaying this water debt in 2020—water that farmers near La Boquilla Dam in Chihuahua, Mexico, desperately needed to sustain their crops. Drought and climate change have also impacted the amount of local water, while the arrival of migrants in the region since NAFTA was signed in 1992 has further exacerbated the water shortage, leaving cities like Tijuana and Ciudad Juárez in need of more drinking water. Consequently, protests against shipping the area's essential water supply to the United States erupted throughout

Chihuahua in early 2020, and Mexican president Andrés Manuel López Obrador sent the National Guard to protect La Boquilla Dam. In September 2020, a group of farmers descended upon the dam, overwhelming the soldiers and seizing control of this vital resource. They did not let any water travel north to the US for over a month.[30] This funneling of water north to fulfill an old agreement constitutes invisible violence that border communities in Mexico continue to endure to this day.

Likewise, contemporary border communities experience invisibilized violence when it comes to the disposal of nuclear waste. Sánchez and Pita's *Lunar Braceros, 2125–2148* acknowledges this violence, presenting a speculative fictional narrative in which major multinational entities have exhausted places to deposit nuclear waste on Earth and so begin sending it to the moon. The novel reflects Myrriah M. Gómez's writing about the ecological devastation brought forth from what she calls the "nuclear industrial complex." Since World War II, the US-Mexico borderlands have been a site of nuclear weapons testing, nuclear waste deposits, and uranium mining, leaving border communities suffering from severe illnesses. Gómez describes this inherent violence as "nuclear colonialism," explaining, "Nuclear colonialism is a neocolonial framework that targets not only Indigenous people but also other ethnic minority groups in poor economic situations that have become disenfranchised because of state occupation of their homelands."[31]

According to the Indigenous organization Women of All Red Nations, nuclear colonialism has caused "a broad range of health problems including higher than average rates of cancer, miscarriages, stillbirths, and childhood death."[32] Their claim is corroborated by a report released by the Environmental Protection Agency (EPA) in November 2011 that states:

> Chronic (long-term) inhalation exposure to uranium and radon in humans may cause respiratory effects, such as chronic lung disease, while radium exposure has resulted in acute leukopenia, anemia, necrosis of the jaw, and other effects. Cancer is the

> major effect of concern from the radionuclides. Radium, via oral exposure, may cause bone, head, and nasal passage tumors in humans, and radon, via inhalation exposure, causes lung cancer in humans. Uranium may cause lung cancer and tumors of the lymphatic and hematopoietic tissues.[33]

However, despite studies that found that Navajo men who worked in the uranium mines in New Mexico were highly likely to have developed lung cancer, the 2011 report asserts that uranium, radon, and radium are not "classified for carcinogenicity."[34] The invisibilization of violence is evident in the toxicity seeping through the Navajo Nation's water supply, sickening its people.

The Cyborg Trope: Dehumanization via Invisibilized Labor

Galtung's tranquil waters of structural violence aptly pertains to the fact that most people residing in wealthy countries like the United States do not question where their goods come from, the working conditions of those laboring to produce these goods, and the violence inflicted upon them by powerful corporations aided by governments. They don't think twice about who assembled the smart phone they use to post on social media, the avocado farmers facing cartel violence while providing Americans with their breakfast, or maquiladora workers suffering discrimination, wage theft, and with the rise of femicides in Mexico, physical harm. Invisibilizing such labor forces along the US-Mexico borderlands—which consist of marginalized, racialized peoples—enables consumers to be oblivious to the human rights violations that serve to increase corporate wealth. The Chicanafuturism texts analyzed in this chapter recognize and uncover the invisibilized violence of money- and power-hungry multinational corporations, using cyborgs to represent the dehumanization of racialized labor forces.

The cyborg is, in Lysa Rivera's words, "the quintessential posthuman hybrid produced at the intersection of technology and humanity." She argues that in Chicanafuturism, the cyborg character is a "colonized subject, one whose labor is extracted by US capitalism at the expense of Fragoso's very humanity," referencing the protagonist in Guillermo Lavín's 1994 short story "Reaching the Shore." Lavín's Fragoso volunteers to be a test subject for a North American leisure company, agreeing to have a virtual reality computer chip placed in his brain. Now a cyborg, Fragoso is dehumanized and, as a mere piece of machinery, his labor is invisibilized. Rivera likens this representation to the dehumanization and invisibilization of transborder labor, particularly maquiladora workers who are viewed as cogs in an assembly line rather than as people that deserve human rights.[35] Like cyborgs, they are just machinery and thus disposable.

Sánchez and Pita employ a version of the cyborg trope to depict a racialized labor force in *Lunar Braceros*. The novel features a group of Chicana and Chicano miners who call themselves Tecos, sent to the moon to build nuclear waste deposit sites. The corporation employing the Tecos promises a large sum of money for their services, as well as a pardon for any legal trouble they face back on Earth. However, once they begin work in the lunar mines, they discover a capsule filled with dead bodies and realize that the corporation murdered the previous mining group and has no intention of bringing them back to Earth. As "low skilled workers," the Tecos are dispensable. They are exploited for their labor and, like machinery, destroyed and disposed of once they are no longer useful. Their invisibilization is twofold, as these racialized laborers are physically isolated from Earth and the rest of humanity, and the violence inflicted upon them—death—remains hidden, buried inside a lunar mine.

The parallels between the fictional Tecos and very real maquiladora workers illuminate dehumanizing conditions south of the US-Mexico border, as the latter are overworked, discriminated against, and tossed aside when they have outlasted their usefulness. Despite many nonessential businesses closing for the sake of public health, maquiladoras have had a resurgence along the US-Mexico borderlands during the COVID-19 pandemic. Issues such as laborers contracting the virus, people in lockdown ordering goods online and thus putting more strain on shipping, and scant storage have disrupted supply chains on a global scale. In response, enormous warehouses that function as fulfillment centers for online orders have opened up in Tijuana. This Tijuana maquiladora boom, described by one report as a "new roaring '20s" for the industry, is a result of US tariff code Section 321 of the Tariff Act of 1930. The code states that corporations do not have to pay tariffs on goods valued under two hundred dollars, which the Obama administration increased to eight hundred dollars. Additionally, these products must "be sent directly to individual customers instead of in bulk," this requirement to be regulated internationally by US Customs and Border Patrol.[36] Between 2019 and 2020, shipments using Section 321 increased by 28 percent. Consequently, there is a rush to build additional fulfillment centers in cities south of the border like Tijuana, particularly in light of the movement for unionization in Amazon fulfillment centers in the United States and nonessential commercial shutdowns due to the pandemic. As mentioned at the beginning of this chapter, maquiladora workers in the *Chronicle* report were dismissed for contracting COVID-19 and not being able to work, and discriminated against simply for having comorbidities that would make them susceptible to severe COVID-19 illness. They were tossed aside and dehumanized.

Another maquiladora that remained open during the beginning of the COVID-19 lockdowns, despite not being an "essential" business, is Gulfstream, a supplier for the Pentagon located in Mexicali, Baja California, that builds "G280 and G550 aircraft (known by the US Air Force as C-37B planes)."[37] A 2022 investigative report found that Baja California was hit hard with COVID-19 infections and deaths early in the pandemic. Compellingly titled "'Queremos Vivir' [We want to live]: The Workers Who Wouldn't Die for the Pentagon," the report revealed, "By May 2020, a local news outlet reported that 432 of the 519 Covid-19 fatalities to date had been workers in *maquiladoras*."[38] When Gulfstream laborers refused to work, resulting in a month-long closure of the maquiladora, the US government intervened and demanded that Gulfstream be categorized as an essential business. At this point in the pandemic, the Mexican government had only extended this categorization to the agricultural industry and medical suppliers. Even so, they relented and forced Gulfstream to reopen, despite the fact that the majority of COVID-19 fatalities were maquiladora workers. This choice to keep the maquiladoras running during a deadly and highly infectious global pandemic is evidence of these workers' dehumanization. Like the Tecos in *Lunar Braceros*, their government views them as disposable cogs in a state-sponsored corporate machine.

Cyborg laborers in *Sleep Dealer* suffer a similar fate. After his family farm is destroyed by a drone and his father killed in the attack, Memo absconds to Tijuana to find work to feed his family. There, he meets Luz on a bus and, noticing the metal nodules on her neck and arms, asks where he can get some. Luz tells Memo to see a *coyotek*—a play on the colloquial term *coyote* describing clandestine smugglers that help migrants enter the United States. But after Memo gets robbed, Luz takes him to her coyotek friend's lab and implants the nodules on Memo herself. He then obtains employment at the Cybracero maquiladora, where all the workers are cyborgs, the nodules all over their bodies connected to labor robots in the United States that the cyborgs control remotely. The work they do consists of "low-skilled" labor: a woman stationed next to Memo is a nanny, caring for American children from afar, while Memo is assigned to a robot building a skyscraper at a construction site.

Cybracero's equipment is incredibly dangerous, which further demonstrates the workers' dehumanization and disposability in the eyes of the corporation. The cyberbraceros (cyborg laborers) are all connected to a router on the ceiling of the room, which in one scene begins to spark fire and electrocutes one of the workers, leaving him unconscious. Memo and another cyberbracero unplug him and the supervisor demands that they help him carry the unconscious man to another room. Immediately after, the supervisor barks at Memo to get back to work, as there are cameras watching their every move. We never learn the unconscious man's fate. In another powerful scene, a large piece of glass is hauled past the robot Memo is controlling at the construction site. He sees his reflection in the glass and it is that of a robot, not a human. The image demonstrates just how invisible Memo truly is; he is a machine, disposable and dehumanized. He does not exist to the consumers of his labor who will eventually work or reside in that skyscraper. North of the border, they live in the tranquil waters of obliviousness, ignorant of the dangerous working conditions and meager wages of cyberbraceros.

This invisibilization of cyborg labor is necessary to ensure the protection of corporate businesses and profits in *Sleep Dealer*. The film highlights this point with the character of Rudy Ramirez, a US resident contracted by Del Rio Water to execute drone strikes against perceived threats to the corporation's dams. It is Ramirez, also a cyborg with nodules, who controls the drone that attacks Memo's home and kills his father. A faceless supervisor orders the strike, accusing Memo of being an "aqua-terrorist" when his rudimentary radio catches one of Ramirez's drone signals. In this way, the film depicts invisibilized warfare vis-à-vis drone pilots and the attacks they are ordered to execute by unknown entities. But Ramirez, filled with guilt over the violence he has implemented for his corporate employer, refuses to remain invisible. Instead, he seeks out Memo in Tijuana and together with Luz, the three break into Cybracero. There, Ramirez connects to his drone and launches a missile to destroy Del Rio Water's dam in Santa Ana Del Rio. He thus chooses to reject the life of an invisible drone pilot who ignores the ramifications of his actions and instead resists a powerful corporate entity. Through Ramirez and the cyborg trope, *Sleep Dealer* brings the invisibilization of warfare led by corporations to the forefront. Moreover, in this speculative fictional narrative, Rivera creates cognitive estrangement in relocating of warfare from the Middle East to the US-Mexico borderlands that generates a borderlands consciousness among his viewers, inciting an understanding that corporate power for drone warfare is a real possibility.

In some ways, this is already true. Ramirez's quest for redemption for executing the violent plans of a faceless corporation is not far from reality. On May 9, 2022, the *New York Times* podcast *The Daily* broadcast a shocking interview with James Klein, a former pilot in the US Air Force drone squadron program. Klein flew Predator and Reaper drones from the Creech Air Force Base in Nevada, operating them through "cockpits that were linked by satellite to drones on the other side of the world."[39] During his first few years in the program, much of Klein's work involved surveilling targets of interest, studying them for weeks using "strict protocols." He explained, "Oh, we have found this network and now we can paint a picture, and we know who's doing what, what's really important. Maybe we don't want to kill all these people. Maybe we want to do something else with these people." Significantly, Klein revealed to interviewer Dave Phillips that he and the other drone pilots did not know who was making decisions about if or when to attack targets, the entity giving orders known to them only as "the customer." The customer could be anyone from the president of the United States to CIA operatives, and "whatever the customer wants, the pilot is supposed to give it to him."[40]

After Klein was transferred to a new squadron, however, he had a customer who demanded that he launch missiles at targets within minutes of observing them. The customer did not abide by strict protocols and drone strikes became more frequent, targeting many more innocent civilians. According to Klein, "A rushed strike might be targeting what people thought was an enemy command post, except it's a school and it's full of civilians or it's a market. Or the car that they thought was carrying the terrorist leader, in fact, was carrying a family."[41] Fearing that he would be ordered to kill more innocent targets, Klein developed depression and insomnia, leading to problems with his family. He ultimately quit the drone squadron and was transferred elsewhere. Although drone pilots are a tight-knit community and generally do not share the details of their experiences, *The Daily* reported that another former drone pilot committed suicide after being charged with drug possession by the military court. As with these Air Force drone pilots, Ramirez's mental health suffers as a result of executing the violent plans of a wealthy corporation, the perpetrators shadowy figures with unknown names and faces. The speculative fiction of *Sleep Dealers* is thus very close to reality, as Rivera generates a borderlands consciousness that exposes invisibilized violence toward vulnerable communities.

The Rag Doll Plagues also employs the cyborg trope to this effect. In book 3, Gregory Revueltas, a descendant of Book I's Gregorio Revueltas, travels throughout the Triple Alliance nation-state, a new country that seems to be an amalgamation of the United States, Mexico, and Canada. Gregory works at a research center on the Los Angeles Mexico City Corridor and also sees patients with his partner, Gabi Chung. Gabi is an ambitious physician who had her arm amputated and replaced with a robotic one, which would increase her chances of obtaining a promotion in a futurist world. Her arm is now "a computerized knowledge bank whose fingertips were laser surgical instruments and knowledge cylinders."[42] In a dehumanizing representation of women in the medical field, Gabi is portrayed as a robot, even as Gregory continuously complains of the "smell of burning flesh" emanating from the stump that connects to her robotic arm. Yet despite pathologizing Gabi for becoming a cyborg to enhance her medical career, Gregory's supervisor says that he too must get a robotic arm within a year if he wishes to remain employed.

Moreover, as Ashley B. Tisdale notes, when the two confront a deadly disease that is becoming an epidemic, Gregory wishes he had Gabi's robotic arm, yearning for its knowledge base rather than for Gabi herself. Indeed, when her robotic arm no longer works and she becomes of no use to Gregory, Gabi dies of electrocution.[43] Her value lies only in her robotic arm; she is dehumanized and invisibilized. Gabi's fate reflects those of all Gregory's female love interests throughout *The Rag Doll Plagues*. As Tisdale argues, these characters are essential, "their bodies propel[ling] each Gregory toward a necessary action in battling each illness; however, they are discarded as their diseased or disabled bodies are cast aside not only in the novel but also in criticism."[44] This representation of cyborg women being valued only for their labor and not their humanity is a revealing commentary on how women of color are treated in the workforce, especially in places like maquiladoras. The maquiladora industry is comprised mostly of women and coupled with the continued rise of femicides in Mexico—with over 491 murders between 2019 and 2021 in Ciudad Juárez alone—it is clear that women's lives are not valued.[45] Their value lies in their productivity and reproductivity; once they are no longer productive, they are discarded, invisible. We see this in the continued impunity that perpetrators of femicide enjoy in Mexico, as well as the continued mistreatment of maquiladora workers.

In addition to this dehumanization of cyborg women, Morales uses the cyborg trope when Gregory ultimately discovers a cure for the deadly disease plaguing the country in book 3. In this future world ravaged by illness, "Mexico City was the most contaminated city of the Triple Alliance," and yet inhabitants of the colony of El Pepenador—the worst offender of waste and "biochemical fires"—are largely healthy.[46] Gregory suspects that their blood has healing properties. He tests his theory on children in El Pepenador who are afflicted with disease and finds that the blood of Mexico City inhabitants does indeed heal them if transfused from male to female and vice versa. Gregory administers this treatment to severely sick people in another colony and it continues to be incredibly successful. Soon, a wealthy family residing in Newport Beach contacts him about their twenty-two-year-old daughter, who has been suffering from lung disease for six months. She shows signs of improvement just a few hours after Gregory transfuses the Mexican blood into her body. Gabi demands to know what is healing all these people and Gregory excitedly replies that he "found a human quantum biological leap, maybe a radical adaptation or even a mutation."[47]

When a deadly plague called Blue Buster breaks out in Los Angeles, the medical authorities sanction Gregory's experimental Mexican blood transfusions. They obtain the healing blood from soldiers stationed in Mexico City: "It was obvious these warriors had a dual purpose. Here, they were the Triple Alliance military force in charge of the quarantine, and they were my official blood supply."[48] One of these Mexican soldiers is taken to the home of a powerful woman, Elena Tarn, for Gregory to transfuse his blood into her ill daughter. When the treatment proves effective, Gregory finds out that Tarn has purchased a Mexican woman (a virgin, in fact) to breed with the soldier, hold the couple at her home, and amass their restorative blood over time: "They would live in privileged enslavement for the remainder of their lives. Their blood was worth lives and Elena Tarn guaranteed herself and her daughter an indefinite supply."[49]

Again, we see the cyborg trope representing the exploitation of marginalized people of color, as the Mexican soldier and his Mexican virgin are treated like dialysis machines, invisibilized as pieces of medical equipment to be used by Elena Tarn and her daughter. There is a borderlands consciousness in the reader of discovering that these two human beings are, as Gregory points out, being kept as functional pets. This also evokes a sense of awareness that, historically, we have seen this before: white people in the United States kept African Americans in bondage for over three hundred years. The phrase "privileged enslavement" is a euphemism—an attempt to make one thing another—which exposes the violence inherent in owning another human being. Attempts to rationalize it only exacerbate the dehumanization, as when Elena Tarn states, "They can go anywhere they desire under the protection of my guards."[50] Justification of violence is also a violent act.

Conclusion

The three Chicanafuturist texts examined here present their audiences with alternate worlds in which the exploitation of and violence against people of color are invisibilized, normalized as components of a functioning society by those who obliviously benefit from their pain. This violence is obvious to the audience, producing cognitive estrangement when faced with a dystopian world at the hands of money- and power-hungry hegemonies. *Lunar Braceros, 2125–2148* depicts reservations filled with people who by virtue of being unemployed or homeless do not participate in a hypercapitalistic society. The authors thereby offer a literary indictment of the treatment of Indigenous communities relegated to reservations after their lands were stolen and subsequently, in the case of the Navajo Nation, poisoned by nuclear colonialism. The working conditions in Cybracero and workers' invisibility to consumers north of the border in *Sleep Dealer* is a denunciation of the mistreatment of maquiladora—of which US consumers remain willfully or unintentionally ignorant. And the purchase of Mexicans as personal dialysis machines in *The Rag Doll Plagues* is an accusation exposing the willingness to dehumanize people of color in the wake of global plague, as we have seen with the maquiladora workers who perished during the COVID-19 pandemic to serve the industrial needs of their neighbor to the north. Uncovering such violence—making what is invisibilized visible—inspires a borderlands consciousness to rise within the audiences of these texts, conjuring connections to sad realities through speculative fiction.

However, borderlands consciousness is not just about raising awareness; it is also about the resistance and resilience of borderlands communities. Breaking through the cognitive estrangement, leading the audience to recognize the parallel violence in our present world, is an act of resistance. The *Lunar Braceros*' escape from death at the hands of a powerful corporation, the destruction of the dam in *Sleep Dealer*, and Mexicans' growing power in the Directorate at the end of *The Rag Doll Plagues* are all examples of Olguín's celebration of Chicanafuturism—cultural productions that "[resist] the nihilist impulse of most postmodernist narratives."[51] There is no room for fatalism in these texts; there is only the call to splash into the tranquil waters of invisibilized violence and create waves of justice.

EPILOGUE

Fibroblast Migration and Borderlands Consciousness

The US-Mexico border has been a part of who I am since I was a young child, and since then I have seen that powerful entities enact violence on this place that is important to me and my community. During my childhood, my family and I would travel from Albuquerque to Ciudad Juárez about twice a month, as my parents would see their dentist, buy some Mexican grocery items not available in the United States, and even get haircuts. Every year in August, my parents would buy our back-to-school clothes in El Paso, and one year for Christmas they bought us bicycles in Ciudad Juárez. As a child, I loved going to Ciudad Juárez; it felt like a minivacation, and my parents were very happy to be in a place in which they felt safe for a couple of days.

However, it was always a scary experience for me as a child to cross back into the United States; the border patrol agents frightened me. One year, after my father became a naturalized citizen of the US, he was ready to answer to border patrol that he was now an American citizen. When our turn came to engage with the border patrol agent, he barked, "Where you from?!" and my father, who speaks English with an accent, answered, "American citizenship." The border patrol agent aggressively asked, "What did you say?" to which my father nervously corrected himself by replying, "Uh, I'm sorry, American citizen." The border patrol then laughed mockingly, demanding to see my dad's paperwork, and finally let us pass. It was a very unsettling experience, and that upset feeling I got in my stomach still comes back whenever I visit the US-Mexico border and see those trucks with the green stripe. By the time I was a teenager in the early 2000s, the femicides were on the news every day and we stopped going to Ciudad Juárez so often. The last time my parents took me there was to buy my quinceañera dress in 2002. Ciudad Juárez was no longer a safe space for my parents or for me as a young woman.

As an adult, I have visited the US-Mexico border on multiple occasions, and each time I have felt a deep sense of connection to this liminal space, as it was where my family had some of our fondest memories. As I wrote in the introduction of this book, violence is not inherent to the people that inhabit the US-Mexico borderlands, as some news media outlets would like society to think. Rather, the violence experienced in the borderlands is manifested by structures that marginalize communities, preventing them from being able to reach their potential. Throughout this book, I continually went back to Johan Galtung's definition of violence: "Violence is that which increases the distance between the potential and the actual, and that which impedes the decrease of this distance." Presented in this book are historical events, contemporary circumstances, policymaking and legislation that inhibit the potential of marginalized communities along the US-Mexico borderlands to create their current actuality. This impediment to their potential is rooted in colonialism, racism, and capitalism: from the healing of impoverished and Indigenous communities by Santa Teresa while the Mexican government sought to take Indigenous lands, to borderlands communities facing land seizure by eminent domain, and migrants fleeing violence only to have the human right of asylum denied. All these groups of people had the potential to live fulfilling lives in which they were safe and tied to their ancestral land, and for their descendants to also have this opportunity, yet were inhibited by colonialism, capitalism, and racism. The distance between this potential and their actuality—that is violence.

The importance of studying how violence—that is, impeding the potential of a community—is paramount in the twenty-first century, as white supremacy and backlash against calls for racial and social justice have grown. Additionally, institutions like the United States Supreme Court have been severely tainted by truly violent rulings in the 2022 season, such as limiting excessive force lawsuits against Border Patrol, removing safeguards against judicial errors, the overturning of *Roe v. Wade*, and upholding the ability to carry concealed weapons. The backlash we have seen in the twenty-first century against antiracist and decolonial efforts has been harsh and heavy; the importance and relevance of having a borderlands consciousness is crucial as we head into a future of climate change that will affect borderlands communities and of unelected officials making policy decisions that will negatively impact Brown and Black populations. The violence our communities will continue to face must not escape us, and we act upon this borderland consciousness by consistently and publicly denouncing this violence. This book, through the study of literature, film, and art, is one way of doing so.

After spending more than two and a half years writing this book, the question of the importance of studying violence represented in literature, film, and art is constant: why should we care about narrative and art of the US-Mexico borderlands produced by inhabitants of the borderlands? Teresa Delgado, theologian and author of *A Puerto Rican Decolonial Theology: Prophesy Freedom* (2017), articulated in a recent interview that her work on decolonizing theology is heavily influenced by Puerto Rican literature: "To me there was a natural connection between using the stories of our people, stories of Puerto Rican artists that were reconstructing places and times and people and ways of being that I couldn't get enough of because I had . . . been severed from that: the colonial project does that."[1] In this same spirit, I chose to include the work of Mexican and Chicanx authors and artists that inhabit the US-Mexico borderlands to tell the story of our land and people, to reconstruct what Delgado explains is the story of our gente because of the violence of colonization that severs us from our history. From the writings of nineteenth-century authors to the mirror artwork installed at the US-Mexico border wall, the cultural production of borderlands communities is crucial to understanding who we are and how we live in this space with dignity. I have argued throughout this book that the borderlands consciousness brought about by Mexican and Chicanx artists' cultural productions of the borderlands brings about a dignified existence that is rooted in resistance, resilience, and love for ourselves, our land, and our communities.

With this book, my intention was never to solely highlight violence of the US-Mexico borderlands but to emphasize and celebrate the borderlands consciousness of our gente and to participate in the healing of being severed from our history that colonialism has wrought. The process of writing this book has included long conversations with my husband, Alfonso, about these topics. As a physician, he connects our discussions to his knowledge of medicine and physiology, and he commented one day, "This work, borderlands consciousness, is like when there is an open wound: in order for the healing process to begin, the cells must cross over. This is called fibroblast migration." He demonstrated this by touching the bottom of the palms of his hands to each other, and then intertwining his fingers from either hand around each other, to then finally clasp his hands together to signify the healing of the wound. This connection he made of an open wound healing through cell migration immediately helped me make the connection to Anzaldúa's metaphor of the US-Mexico borderlands being an "open wound," and how she concludes *Borderlands* with a celebration of día de la Chicana and Chicano. She describes that day as one in which she "[affirms] who we are ... [and searches] for our essential dignity as a people, people with a sense of purpose—to belong and contribute to something greater than our *pueblo*."[2] I truly believe that this celebration is that border communities, los fronterizos, those who cross borders, are the healers of our wounds caused by the violence discussed in this book. We are the healers through the love we hold for our communities, the fight we bring to defend our lives and environment, and the bravery to cross borders. These healing properties in the face of hegemonic violence are the fibroblast migration that ties us together, sucks out the infected purulence that is colonialism, capitalism, and racism, and brings about dignity and life. Borderlands consciousness is a healing property, a salve for our gente fronteriza, that we must embrace as we continue into the twenty-first century.

NOTES

Introduction

1. In this book I will be using the terms *Latinx* and *Chicanx* as they are inclusive terms for all persons, including those who are gender nonconforming.
2. Anzaldúa, *Borderlands / La Frontera*, 56.
3. Saldívar, *Border Matters*, 19.
4. Chabram-Dernersesian, "Introduction," 180.
5. Saldívar, *Border Matters*, 19.
6. Sandoval, *Methodology of the Oppressed*, 72–73.
7. Sandoval, *Methodology of the Oppressed*, 73.
8. Galtung, "Violence, Peace, and Peace Research," 168–69.
9. Galtung, "Violence, Peace, and Peace Research," 168.
10. Galtung, "Violence, Peace, and Peace Research," 171.
11. Galtung, "Violence, Peace, and Peace Research," 170.
12. Guidotti-Hernández, *Unspeakable Violence*, 1–2.
13. Saldívar, *Border Matters*, 17.
14. Saldívar, *Border Matters*, 9, 57.
15. Johnson quoted in Saldívar, *Border Matters*, 26–27.
16. Rosaldo, *Culture and Truth*, 26.
17. Zobl and Klaus, "Cultural Production."
18. I attribute this characterization of my work to Natalia M. Toscano.

Chapter One

1. Vanderwood, *Power of God*, 159.
2. Vanderwood, *Power of God*, 226.
3. Galtung, "Violence, Peace, and Peace Research," 169.
4. Martin, *Borderlands Saints*, 34.
5. Vanderwood, *Power of God*, 163–64.

6. Vanderwood, *Power of God*, 168.
7. Vanderwood, *Power of God*, 168–72.
8. Seman, *Borderlands Curanderos*, 23.
9. Liberation theology is the theological approach and teaching that scripture uplifts the oppressed and includes calls for social justice for the poor and disenfranchised. While the idea of liberation theology came about officially in 1968 in the Latin American Bishops' Conference in Medellín, Colombia, Teresa Urrea employed much of its central tenets in her own theology and teachings.
10. Vanderwood, "Santa Teresa," 215.
11. Vanderwood, *Power of God*, 198.
12. Gutiérrez and Young, "Transnationalizing Borderlands History."
13. Pérez, *Decolonial Imaginary*, 26.
14. Vasconcelos, *La Raza Cósmica*.
15. Johnson, "Cosmic Race in Texas," 404–19.
16. Urrea, *Hummingbird's Daughter*, 498.
17. Vanderwood, *Power of God*, 164–65.
18. Robinson, "From Private Healer," 262.
19. Robinson, "From Private Healer," 241–42.
20. Urrea, *Hummingbird's Daughter*, 352.
21. Vanderwood, *Power of God*, 169–71.
22. Vanderwood, *Power of God*, 171–78.
23. Urrea, *Hummingbird's Daughter*, 353–54.
24. Urrea, *Hummingbird's Daughter*, 353–54.
25. Holden, *Teresita*, 125.
26. Urrea, *Hummingbird's Daughter*, 356.
27. Urrea, *Hummingbird's Daughter*, 356.
28. Urrea, *Hummingbird's Daughter*, 362.
29. Vanderwood, *Power of God*, 146.
30. Conger, "Díaz and Church Hierarchy," 241.
31. Urrea, *Hummingbird's Daughter*, 235–36.
32. Urrea, *Hummingbird's Daughter*, 417–19.
33. Urrea, *Hummingbird's Daughter*, 356.
34. Holden, *Teresita*, 125–26.
35. Hu-Dehart, "Development and Rural Rebellion," 89.

36. Saldaña-Portillo, *Indian Given*, 154.
37. Hu-Dehart, "Development and Rural Rebellion," 90.
38. Hu-Dehart, "Development and Rural Rebellion," 90.
39. Hu-Dehart, "Development and Rural Rebellion," 84.
40. Hu-Dehart, "Development and Rural Rebellion," 77.
41. Hu-Dehart, "Development and Rural Rebellion," 88.
42. See Pulido, "Geographies of Race."
43. Hu-Dehart, "Development and Rural Rebellion," 83.
44. Guidotti-Hernandez, *Unspeakable Violence*, 180.
45. Hu-Dehart, "Development and Rural Rebellion," 83.
46. Urrea, *Hummingbird's Daughter*, 266.
47. Urrea, *Hummingbird's Daughter*, 266.
48. Urrea, *Hummingbird's Daughter*, 266.
49. Urrea, *Hummingbird's Daughter*, 478.
50. Boyd, "Twenty Years to Nogales," 298.
51. Pulido, "Geographies of Race," 314.
52. Nava, "Teresa Urrea," 500.
53. Urrea, *Hummingbird's Daughter*, 375.
54. Urrea, *Hummingbird's Daughter*, 376–77.
55. Urrea, *Hummingbird's Daughter*, 377.

Chapter Two

1. Cecilia Rasmussen, "Protester May Have Been Railroaded," *Los Angeles Times*, February 1, 2004, https://www.latimes.com/archives/la-xpm-2004-feb-01-me-then1-story.html.
2. Robinson, *Land in California*, 100.
3. US General Accounting Office, *Treaty of Guadalupe Hidalgo*.
4. Robinson, *Land in California*, 101.
5. Robinson, *Land in California*, 14.
6. Miller, "Secret Treaties," 39.
7. Orsi, *Sunset Limited*, 5.
8. Van Metre, *Transportation in the United States*, 43.

9. Pacific Railway Act of 1862, Pub. L. No. 12, Stat. 489 (1862).
10. Robinson, *Land in California*, 150.
11. Robinson, *Land in California*, 147.
12. Robinson, *Land in California*, 151.
13. Robinson, *Land in California*, 151.
14. Robinson, *Land in California*, 157.
15. Robinson, *Land in California*, 151.
16. A hacendado was the owner of a large estate called a *hacienda* that employed *peones* (essentially involuntary servants), many of whom were Indigenous.
17. Payen-Variéras, "Gilded-Age Entrepreneurs," 3.
18. Payen-Variéras, "Gilded-Age Entrepreneurs," 4.
19. Orsi, *Sunset Limited*, 22.
20. George C. Werner, "Texas and Pacific Railway," *Handbook of Texas Online*, updated July 16, 2016, https://www.tshaonline.org/handbook/entries/texas-and-pacific-railway.
21. Ruiz de Burton, *Squatter and the Don*, 313.
22. Ruiz de Burton, *Squatter and the Don*, 316.
23. Ruiz de Burton, *Squatter and the Don*, 316.
24. Smythe, *History of San Diego*, part 3, chapter 3.
25. Ruiz de Burton, *Squatter and the Don*, 318.
26. Ruiz de Burton, *Squatter and the Don*, 365.
27. Santa Clara County v. Southern Pacific Railroad Company, 118 U.S. 394 (1885).
28. Cited in Ruiz de Burton, *Squatter and the Don*, 367 (emphasis added).
29. John M. González, "Whiteness of the Blush," 162.
30. Berger, "Surveying the Golden State," 212.
31. González, "Whiteness of the Blush," 163.
32. Kanellos, Introduction, 1.
33. Garcílazo, *Traqueros*, 34.
34. Garcílazo, *Traqueros*, 11.
35. Bracken, "Borderland Biopolitics," 32.
36. Kanellos, Introduction, 1.
37. Venegas, *Don Chipote*, 35.
38. Venegas, *Don Chipote*, 35.
39. Venegas, *Don Chipote*, 35.

40. Bracken, "Borderlands Biopolitics," 31; Venegas, *Don Chipote*, 36.
41. Bracken, "Borderlands Biopolitics," 31.
42. Venegas, *Don Chipote*, 36.
43. Stern, *Eugenic Nation*, 58.
44. Fallon, "Staging a Protest," 117–18.
45. Venegas, *Don Chipote*, 59.
46. Venegas, *Don Chipote*, 59.
47. Venegas, *Don Chipote*, 59.
48. Venegas, *Don Chipote*, 78.
49. Venegas, *Don Chipote*, 70–71.
50. Garcílazo, *Traqueros*, 65.
51. Garcílazo, *Traqueros*, 66.

Chapter Three

1. Wiesel, "The Refugee," 388.
2. Immigration and Nationality Act, 8 U.S.C. § 1101(a)(42)(A) (1995).
3. Immigration and Nationality Act, 8 U.S.C. § 1157.
4. Immigration and Nationality Act, 8 U.S.C. § 1158.
5. Bureau of Population, Refugees, and Migration, *Report to Congress*.
6. UN High Commissioner for Refugees, *Convention and Protocol*, 3.
7. UN General Assembly, Resolution 217, Universal Declaration of Human Rights, A/RES/217 (December 10, 1948), https://www.un.org/en/about-us/universal-declaration-of-human-rights.
8. Galtung, "Violence, Peace, and Peace Research," 172.
9. Hing, "Mistreating Central American Refugees," 359.
10. Thomas Jefferson et al., Declaration of Independence, July 4, 1776, https://www.archives.gov/founding-docs/declaration-transcript.
11. Musalo, "El Salvador," 231.
12. Trina Realmuto, "ABC v. Thornburgh: 20 Years Later," National Immigration Project, January 31, 2011, 2, https://www.nationalimmigrationproject.org/PDFs/practitioners/practice_advisories/gen/2011_31Jan_abc-20-years.pdf, accessed June 9, 2022.
13. Realmuto, "ABC v. Thornburgh," 2.
14. Musalo, "El Salvador," 184.

15. Commission for Historical Clarification, "Guatemala—Memory of Silence," 543.
16. Kelli Lyon-Johnson, "Acts of War," 206–7.
17. Martínez, *Confessions*, 4.
18. Martínez, *Mother Tongue*, 6.
19. Nolan-Ferrel, "Pedimos Posada," 171.
20. Martínez, *Confessions*, 121–22.
21. Martínez, *Confessions*, 122.
22. Martínez, *Confessions*, 122.
23. Chapablanco, "Traveling While Hispanic," 1402.
24. Chapablanco, "Traveling While Hispanic," 1420.
25. Chapablanco, "Traveling While Hispanic," 1408.
26. Chapablanco, "Traveling While Hispanic," 1409.
27. Martínez, *Confessions*, 120.
28. Martínez, *Mother Tongue*, 54–55.
29. Goldsmith et al., "Ethno-Racial Profiling," 97.
30. Esses, Medianu, and Lawson, "Uncertainty," 519.
31. Martínez, *Mother Tongue*, 33.
32. "No More Deaths: An Interview with John Fife," *Reflections*, Yale Divinity School (Fall 2008), https://reflections.yale.edu/article/who-my-neighbor-facing-immigration/no-more-deaths-interview-john-fife.
33. Martínez, *Confessions*, 110.
34. Paik, "Abolitionist Futures," 6.
35. Martínez, "Nativity," 132.

Chapter Four

1. Pérez, "El desorden," 19.
2. Anzaldúa, *Borderlands / La Frontera*, 153.
3. The use of the verb *theologize* is purposeful as it is defined as "engage in theological reasoning or speculation" in the Oxford English Dictionary. This act of engaging is transgressive for a woman, particularly with a Catholic priest, as the gendered hierarchies are delineated to prescribe male authority over all theological questions. See Raab, *When Women Become Priests*.
4. Castillo, *So Far from God*, 23.

5. Castillo, *So Far from God*, 23.
6. Escandón, *Esperanza's Box of Saints*, 244.
7. Escandón, *Esperanza's Box of Saints*, 244–45.
8. Alarcón, Kaplan, and Moallem, "Introduction," 1.
9. Alarcón, Kaplan, and Moallem, "Introduction," 2.
10. Mohanty, *Feminism without Borders*, 1–2.
11. Johnson, "Covert Wars," 159.
12. Johnson, "Covert Wars," 157.
13. Penitentes are a "lay Catholic penitential brotherhood of New Mexican flagellants, who long have called themselves Los Hermanos de Nuestro Padre Jesus Nazareno" and have existed since the eighteenth century. J. Manuel Espinosa explains that their most important purpose is "to commemorate the Passion and Death of Christ during the Lenten season and especially during Holy Week" by flagellating themselves, carrying large wooden crosses, and even wrapping cacti around their bodies to perform the "disciplinas" of their rituals. See Espinosa, "Origin of Penitentes," 1–2.
14. Alarcón, "Chicana Feminism," 68.
15. Definition of trafficking: "The recruitment, transportation, transfer, harbouring or receipt of persons, by means of the threat or use of force or other forms of coercion, of abduction, of fraud, of deception, of the abuse of power or of a position of vulnerability or of the giving or receiving of payments or benefits to achieve the consent of a person having control over another person, for the purpose of exploitation. Exploitation shall include, at a minimum, the exploitation of the prostitution of others or other forms of sexual exploitation, forced labour or services, slavery or practices similar to slavery, servitude or the removal of organs." See UN General Assembly, Resolution 55/25, Protocol to Prevent, Suppress and Punish Trafficking in Persons, A/RES/55/25 (November 15, 2000), https://www.ohchr.org/en/professionalinterest/pages/protocoltraffickinginpersons.aspx.
16. UN Office on Drugs and Crime, *Report on Trafficking*, 22.
17. Escandón, *Esperanza's Box of Saints*, 49.
18. Some Protestant denominations also prescribe roles and expectations regarding gender, but with different theological bases than Catholicism.
19. Although the Roman Catholic Church is categorized under the inclusive term *Christianity*, Catholicism must not be confused with Protestant Christian denominations, many of which do allow women to take on leadership roles.

According to the Pew Research Center, the Protestant denominations that do not allow female leadership at an executive level (pastoral, deaconry) are the Church of Jesus Christ of Latter-Day Saints (Mormons), the Missouri Synod Lutheran Church, and the Southern Baptist Convention. In addition, even though it is not Protestant or Catholic, the Orthodox Church of America is Christian but also does not allow female leadership. See David Maschi, "The Divide over Ordaining Women," *Fact Tank: New in the* Numbers, Pew Research Center, last modified September 9, 2014, www.pewresearch.org/fact-tank/2014/09/09/the-divide-over-ordaining-women/.

20. Raab, *When Women Become Priests*, 39.

21. These documents are Declaration *Inter Insigniores* on the Question of Admission of Women to the Ministerial Priesthood (1976), which contains "four drafts of a pastoral letter on women" and an apostolic letter written by Pope John Paul II in 1994 titled *Ordinatio Sacerdotalis*. See Raab, *When Women Become Priests*, 27–30.

22. Raab, *When Women Become Priests*, 36.

23. Thomas Aquinas (1225–1274) was an Italian Dominican theologian whose teachings were, and continue to be, influential in Catholic doctrine. He wrote *Summa Theologica*, which contains most of the teachings of Christianity and five famous arguments supporting the existence of God. Aquinas was canonized July 18, 1323, by Pope John XXII. See Robert Pasnau, "Thomas Aquinas," *Stanford Encyclopedia of Philosophy (Spring 2023 Edition)*, https://plato.stanford.edu/entries/aquinas.

24. Aquinas, *Summa Theologica*, part 3, supplement, question 39, article 1.

25. Segura and Pesquera, "Beyond Indifference and Antipathy," 72.

26. Segura and Pesquera, "Beyond Indifference and Antipathy," 73.

27. Anzaldúa, *Borderlands / La Frontera*, 58.

28. Many Chicana feminists have theorized and posited that Malinche, being a slave to the Mayans and subsequently to Hernán Cortés, used her ability of speech to survive her oppressive situation. Chicana literature thus paints Malinche as a visionary who saw beyond her circumstances. La Llorona is also a figure that has been reappropriated by Chicana feminists. While she is not a historical figure like Malinche, La Llorona has been represented as a murderous mother seeking revenge, eternally searching for her dead children, and is a well-known folkloric cautionary tale. Chicana feminists have taken the vituperative representation of La Llorona to theorize how a woman in dire circumstances will look for her lost children as long

as it takes. She will be transgressive and commit taboo acts in order to find them. See Anzaldúa, *Borderlands / La Frontera*.

29. Schoeffel, *Maternal Conditions*, 46.
30. Castillo, *So Far from God*, 28.
31. Aurelio M. Espinosa writes about la malogra in Nuevomexicano folklore: "The myth about the evil one, *la malora* (*mala hora*), also pronounced *malogra* (literally, 'the evil hour'), is indeed interesting, both from the purely folk-lore side as well as from the philological side. How mala hora, the evil hour, ill fate, bad luck, came to be thought of as a definite concrete idea of an individual wicked spirit, is interesting from more than one point of view. This myth is a well-known one. *La malora* is an evil spirit which wanders about in the darkness of the night at the cross-roads and other places. It terrorizes the unfortunate ones who wander alone at night, and has usually the form of a large lock of wool or the whole fleece of wool of a sheep (*un vellón de lana*). Sometimes it takes a human form, but this is rare; and the New Mexicans say that when it has been seen in human form, it presages ill fate, death, or the like. When it appears on dark nights in the shape of a fleece of wool, it diminishes and increases in size in the very presence of the unfortunate one who sees it. It is also generally believed that a person who sees la malora, like one who sees a ghost (*un difunto*), forever remains senseless. When asked for detailed information about this myth, the New Mexicans give the general reply, 'It is an evil thing' (*es cosa mala*)." Espinosa, "New-Mexican Spanish Folk-Lore," 400.
32. Castillo, *So Far from God*, 39.
33. Castillo, *So Far from God*, 39.
34. Castillo, *So Far from God*, 32.
35. Cervantes Saavedra, *Don Quijote*, 93, 113–15.
36. La Llorona "is a figure of mourning that weeps for the losses Chicanas and Chicanos have sustained in contemporary mainstream American culture, especially women, who suffer gender as well as ethnic oppression. *She is, at the same time, a figure of revolt against those same losses*" (emphasis mine). Perez, *There Was a Woman*, 35.
37. hooks, *Yearning*, 41.
38. Maringer, "Priests and Priestesses," 101.
39. Sandoval, *Methodology of the Oppressed*, 139.
40. Rabuzzi, *Sacred and the Feminine*, 43.

41. Etymological history of *home*: "Despite the fact that home is a concept deeply embedded in our thinking, no distinct word exists for it in classical Greek or ancient Hebrew.... Despite the absence of a separate word to distinguish it from the closely related house, the underlying idea is implicit at times in classical Greek. For instance, it sometimes attaches to the word 'family' (oikia, oikikos), as occurs in the Septuagint, the Greek translation of the Old Testament." Rabuzzi, *Sacred and the Feminine*, 44.

42. Rabuzzi, *Sacred and the Feminine*, 55–56.

43. Castillo, *So Far from God*, 55.

44. Castillo, *So Far from God*, 138.

45. Escandón, *Esperanza's Box of Saints*, 76.

46. Sandoval, *Methodology of the Oppressed*, 142.

47. John 10:11 (New International Version).

48. A *limpia* is "a ritual sweeping designed to protect a person from harm, to remove bad influences, and to provide spiritual strength." See Trotter and Chavira, *Curanderismo*, 181.

49. Pérez, *Chicana Art*, 20.

50. Philip Bump, "Hundreds of Immigrant Families Split Apart under Trump Remain Separated," *Washington Post*, February 13, 2023, https://www.washingtonpost.com/politics/2023/02/13/trump-immigrants-children-border/.

51. In August 2016, Pope Francis announced that he would establish a commission for the study of deaconship for women, comprised of six men and six women. The announcement indicates that the commission's purpose is to consider the calling of deaconship for women "especially with regard to the first ages of the Church." See "Pope Institutes Commission to Study the diaconate of Women," *Vatican Radio*, updated August 2, 2016, http://www.archivioradiovaticana.va/storico/2016/08/02/pope_institutes_commission_to_study_the_diaconate_of_women/en-1248731.

Chapter Five

1. Amber Phillips, "'They're Rapists.' President Trump's Campaign Launch Speech Two Years Later, Annotated," *Washington Post*, June 16, 2017, https://www.washingtonpost.com/news/the-fix/wp/2017/06/16/theyre-rapists-presidents-trump-campaign-launch-speech-two-years-later-annotated/.

2. Galtung, "Violence, Peace, and Peace Research," 169.

3. La Cueva Salcedo, "Environmental Violence," 22.

4. "Border Brujo: 1988 to 1989," *Essential Works: A Gómez-Peña Project Chronology*, on Guillermo Gómez-Peña's official website, accessed November 1, 2021, https://www.guillermogomezpena.com/works/#border-brujo.

5. Keller, *Contemporary Chicana and Chicano Art*, 44.

6. Anzaldúa, *Borderlands / La Frontera*, 106–7.

7. Anzaldúa, *Borderlands / La Frontera*, 113.

8. Guillermo Gómez-Peña, "On the Other Side of the Mexican Mirror," *Pocha Nostra*, accessed November 5, 2021, http://www.pochanostra.com/antes/jazz_pocha2/mainpages/otherside.htm.

9. Matthew Harrison Tedford, "Ana Teresa Fernández Erases the US-Mexico Border," *Sculpture Nature*, January 20, 2017, https://www.sculpturenature.com/en/ana-teresa-fernandez-erases-the-u-s-mexico-border/.

10. Fernández quoted in Matt Stromberg, "For Artists, the US-Mexico Border Is Fertile Territory," *Artsy*, March 6, 2017, https://www.artsy.net/article/artsy-editorial-mexican-artists-threat-trumps-wall-fuel-inspiration.

11. "About Us." Santa Ana National Wildlife Refuge, US Fish and Wildlife Service, accessed June 29, 2022, https://www.fws.gov/refuge/santa-ana/about-us.

12. Carlos Sanchez, "Is the Santa Ana Wildlife Refuge Still in the Crosshairs of Trump's Border Wall?" *Texas Monthly*, August 30, 2019, https://www.texasmonthly.com/news-politics/santa-ana-wildlife-refuge-trump-border-wall/.

13. C. Sanchez, "Santa Ana Wildlife Refuge."

14. Sandra Sanchez, "Building a Border Wall in South Texas," *NBC4i*, last modified September 18, 2019, https://www.nbc4i.com/border-report-tour/building-a-border-wall-in-south-texas/.

15. Center for Biological Diversity, "Trump Administration Waives Environmental Laws to Build Border Walls in New Mexico, Arizona," press release, April 23, 2019, https://www.biologicaldiversity.org/news/press_releases/2019/border-wall-environmental-laws-04-23-2019.php.

16. Michel Marizco, "Archaeologists Say Border Wall Cuts through Native American Burial Sites in Arizona," *All Things Considered*, NPR, February 19, 2020, https://www.npr.org/2020/02/19/807488196/archaeologists-say-border-wall-cuts-through-native-american-burial-sites-in-ariz.

17. Charlie McDonald, "Saguaro (*Carnegiea gigantea*)," US Department of Agriculture, accessed August 18, 2020, https://www.fs.usda.gov/wildflowers/plant-of-the-week/carnegiea_gigantea.shtml.

18. "Native Burial Sites Blown up for US Border Wall," *BBC News*, February 10, 2020, https://www.bbc.com/news/world-us-canada-51449739.

19. Treaty of Guadalupe Hidalgo, U.S.-Mexico, February 2,1848, *National Archives*, https://www.archives.gov/milestone-documents/treaty-of-guadalupe-hidalgo.

20. Eli Saslow, "Trump's Border Wall Threatens to End Texas Family's 250 Years of Ranching on Rio Grande," *Washington Post*, September 8, 2018, https://www.washingtonpost.com/national/trumps-border-wall-threatens-to-end-texas-families-250-years-of-ranching-on-rio-grande/2018/09/08/92e721d2-b12d-11e8-a20b-5f4f84429666_story.html.

21. John Burnett, "Between President Trump's Border Wall and the Rio Grande Lies a 'No Man's Land,'" *Morning Edition*, NPR, February 14, 2020, https://www.npr.org/2020/02/14/805239927/between-president-trumps-border-wall-and-the-rio-grande-lies-a-no-man-s-land.

22. Samuel Gilbert, "Pandemic Fears in Border Towns as Workers Flock in to Build Trump's Wall," *Guardian*, April 16, 2020, https://www.theguardian.com/environment/2020/apr/16/trump-border-wall-coronavirus-pandemic-ajo-arizona.

23. Gilbert, "Pandemic Fears."

24. Gilbert, "Pandemic Fears."

25. Molly Hennessy-Fiske, "Trump Accelerates Border Wall Construction Ahead of Election, Despite Pandemic," *Los Angeles Times*, June 30, 2020, https://www.latimes.com/world-nation/story/2020-06-30/trump-accelerates-border-wall-construction-ahead-of-election-despite-pandemic.

26. These are figures from US Census Bureau, American Community Survey, 2018, https://www.census.gov/programs-surveys/acs.

27. Richard A. Oppel Jr. et al., "The Fullest Look Yet at the Racial Inequity of Coronavirus," *New York Times*, July 5, 2020, https://www.nytimes.com/interactive/2020/07/05/us/coronavirus-latinos-african-americans-cdc-data.html.

28. "Nogales City, Arizona Census Quick Facts 2020," United States Census Bureau, https://www.census.gov/quickfacts/nogalescityarizona; "Ajo, AZ," Census Reporter, https://censusreporter.org/profiles/16000US0400870-ajo-az/.

29. Gilbert, "Pandemic Fears."

30. Regulations to Control Communicable Diseases, 42 U.S.C. § 264.

31. Uriel J. García, "Here's What You Need to Know about Title 42, the Pandemic-Era Policy That Quickly Sends Migrants to Mexico," *Texas Tribune*, April 19, 2022, https://www.texastribune.org/2022/04/29/immigration-title-42-biden/.

32. Ronald Rael (@rrael), Instagram photo caption, July 29, 2019, https://www.instagram.com/p/B0fY2R6hfKr/.

33. Joshua Barajas, "Why This Artist Used Seesaws to Protest at the Border," *PBS NewsHour*, August 16, 2019, https://www.pbs.org/newshour/arts/pink-seesaws-at-the-border-wall-showed-that-play-is-a-form-of-protest.

Chapter Six

1. "Three Factors Contributing to the Ongoing Global Supply-Chain Crisis," *Fuqua Insights*, Fuqua School of Business, Duke University, December 13, 2021, https://www.fuqua.duke.edu/duke-fuqua-insights/robert-swinney-three-factors-contributing-ongoing-global-supply-chain-crisis.

2. Erika Carlos, "COVID Factories: The Workers behind the US-Mexico Medical Device Supply Chain," *San Francisco Chronicle*, December 26, 2021, https://www.sfchronicle.com/california/article/coronavirus-medical-device-workers-industry-mexico-16633131.php.

3. "Mexico: Country Commercial Guide," International Trade Administration, US Department of Commerce, last updated September 2, 2021, https://www.trade.gov/country-commercial-guides/mexico-healthcare-products-services.

4. Carlos, "COVID Factories."

5. Steger and Roy, *Neoliberalism*, 5.

6. Steger and Roy, *Neoliberalism*, 7.

7. Steger and Roy, *Neoliberalism*, 10.

8. Steger and Roy, *Neoliberalism*, 12.

9. Galtung, "Violence, Peace, and Peace Research," 173–74.

10. Ramírez, "Deus ex Machina," 77–78.

11. Olguín, "Contrapuntal Cyborgs?" 129.

12. Uzendoski, "Right to Health," 250–51.

13. Uzendoski, "Right to Health," 251.

14. Lavender, *Race in American Science Fiction*, 52.
15. Rivera, "Future Histories and Cyborg Labor," 416.
16. Herrera-Sobek, "Epidemics, Epistemophilia, and Racism," 101.
17. Morales, *Rag Doll Plagues*, 16.
18. Morales, *Rag Doll Plagues*, 22.
19. Morales, *Rag Doll Plagues*, 27.
20. Morales, *Rag Doll Plagues*, 26.
21. Herrera-Sobek, "Epidemics, Epistemophilia, and Racism," 101.
22. Morales, *Rag Doll Plagues*, 40.
23. Morales, *Rag Doll Plagues*, 21.
24. The American Medical Association released a statement on November 17, 2020, directly addressing social determinants of health—defined as "economic stability, neighborhood, access to transportation, education and life opportunities, access to food, quality and safety of housing, community/social support, and access to health care"—and the need for a comprehensive approach to manage these inequities. Andis Robeznieks, "'All-Hands-On-Deck Approach' Needed on Social Determinants of Health," American Medical Association, November 17, 2020, https://www.ama-assn.org/delivering-care/health-equity/all-hands-deck-approach-needed-social-determinants-health.
25. Seman, *Borderlands Curanderos*, 88.
26. Seman, *Borderlands Curanderos*, 118.
27. Seman, *Borderlands Curanderos*, 61, 117.
28. Johnson, "Excess of Visibility," 192.
29. Treaty for the Utilization of Waters of the Colorado and Tijuana Rivers and of the Rio Grande, U.S.-Mexico, February 3, 1944, T.S. 994, https://www.ibwc.gov/Files/1944Treaty.pdf; Natalie Kitroeff, "'This Is a War': Cross-Border Fight Over Water Erupts in Mexico," *New York Times*, October 14, 2020, https://www.nytimes.com/2020/10/14/world/americas/mexico-water-boquilla-dam.html.
30. Pamela Constable, "Mexican Farmers Occupy Dam to Stop Water Payments to the United States," *Washington Post*, September 14, 2020, https://www.washingtonpost.com/world/the_americas/us-mexico-water-dam-farm-protest/2020/09/13/dddb85e8-f3bb-11ea-999c-67ff7bf6a9d2_story.html.
31. Gómez, "Toward a Chola Consciousness," 501.

32. Bolton and Unger, "Barren Lands," 373.
33. US Environmental Protection Agency, *Legacy of Uranium Mines*, 3.
34. Gilliland et al., "Uranium Mining," 278–83; US Environmental Protection Agency, "Navajo Nation: Cleaning Up Abandoned Uranium Mines; Health Effects of Uranium," last updated August 5, 2021, https://www.epa.gov/navajo-nation-uranium-cleanup.
35. Rivera, "Future Histories and Cyborg Labor," 420–21.
36. Gustavo Solis, "Resurgent Maquiladoras Are Making Tijuana a Boom Town All Over Again," *KPBS*, January 5, 2022, https://www.kpbs.org/news/border-immigration/2022/01/05/resurgent-maquiladoras-are-making-tijuana-a-boom-town-all-over-again.
37. Maurizio Guerrero, "'Queremos Vivir': The Workers Who Wouldn't Die for the Pentagon," *In These Times*, February 24, 2022, https://inthesetimes.com/article/workerstrike-bordercity-pandemic-mexicali-manquiladoras-how-workers-fought-against-weapons-companies-workers-rights-covid19.
38. Guerrero, "Queremos Vivir."
39. Dave Phillips, "The Unseen Trauma of America's Drone Pilots," *Daily Podcast*, May 9, 2022, https://www.nytimes.com/2022/05/09/podcasts/the-daily/drones-airstrikes-military-ptsd.html?showTranscript=1.
40. James Klein in Phillips, "America's Drone Pilots."
41. Klein in Phillips, "America's Drone Pilots."
42. Morales, *Rag Doll Plagues*, 136.
43. Tisdale, "Transfigured Women," 107.
44. Tisdale, "Transfigured Women," 96.
45. Julian Resendiz, "Juarez Reports Nearly 500 Women Murdered in Past 3 Years," *Border Report*, August 31, 2021, https://www.borderreport.com/hot-topics/border-crime/juarez-reports-nearly-500-women-murdered-in-past-3-years/.
46. Morales, *Rag Doll Plagues*, 164.
47. Morales, *Rag Doll Plagues*, 180.
48. Morales, *Rag Doll Plagues*, 186.
49. Morales, *Rag Doll Plagues*, 193.
50. Morales, *Rag Doll Plagues*, 193.
51. Olguín, "Contrapuntal Cyborgs?" 129.

Epilogue

1. "Re-membering Puerto Ricans," *Mestizo Podcast*, June 15, 2022, https://www.worldoutspoken.com/podcasts/the-mestizo-podcast/s3e7-re-membering-puerto-ricans.
2. Anzaldúa, *Borderlands / La Frontera*, 158.

BIBLIOGRAPHY

Alarcón, Norma. "Chicana Feminism: In the Tracks of 'The' Native Woman." In Kaplan, Alarcón, and Moallem, *Between Woman and Nation*, 63–71.

Alarcón, Norma, Caren Kaplan, and Minoo Moallem. "Introduction: Between Woman and Nation" In Kaplan, Alarcón, and Moallem, *Between Woman and Nation*, 1–16.

Anzaldúa, Gloria. *Borderlands / La Frontera: A New Mestiza*. Critical edition. San Francisco: Aunt Lute Books, 2021.

Aquinas, Thomas. *Summa Theologica*. Translated by Fathers of the English Dominican Province. New York: Benziger Brothers, 1947. www.sacred-texts.com/chr/aquinas/summa/.

Berger, Kayley. "Surveying the Golden State (1850–2020): Vagrancy, Racial Exclusion, Sit-Lie, and the Right to Exist in Public," *California Legal History* 16 (2021): 209–36.

Bolton, Marie, and Nancy C. Unger, "Barren Lands and Barren Bodies in Navajo Nation: Indian Women WARN about Uranium, Genetics, and Sterilization." In *Medicine and Health Care in the Countryside: Historical Approaches and Contemporary Challenges*, edited by Marie Bolton, Patrick Fournier, and Claude Grimmer, 373–92. Bern: Peter Lang, 2019.

Boyd, Consuelo. "Twenty Years to Nogales: The Building of the Guaymas-Nogales Railroad." *Journal of Arizona History* 22, no. 3 (1981): 295–324.

Bracken, Rachel Conrad. "Borderland Biopolitics: Public Health and Border Enforcement in Early Twentieth-Century Latinx Fiction." *English Language Notes* 56, no. 2 (October 2018): 28–43. https://doi.org/10.1215/00138282-6960702.

Bureau of Population, Refugees, and Migration. *Report to Congress on Proposed Refugee Admissions for Fiscal Year 2021*. https://www.state.gov/reports/report-to-congress-on-proposed-refugee-admissions-for-fy-2021/.

Castillo, Ana. *So Far from God: A Novel*. New York: W. W. Norton, 1993.

Cervantes Saavedra, Miguel de. *El Ingenioso Hidalgo Don Quijote de La Mancha*. Dictionary edition. Edited by Thomas A. Lathrop. Cervantes and Co. Spanish Classics: No. 1. Newark, DE: European Masterpieces, 2018.

Chabram-Dernersesian, Angie. "Introduction: Chicana/o and Latina/o Cultural Studies: Transnational and Transdisciplinary Movements." *Cultural Studies* 13, no. 2 (1999): 173–94.

Chapablanco, Pablo, "Traveling While Hispanic: Border Patrol Immigration Investigatory Stops at TSA Checkpoints and Hispanic Appearance." *Cornell Law Review* 104, no. 5 (July 2019): 1401–56. https://scholarship.law.cornell.edu/clr/vol104/iss5/5.

Commission for Historical Clarification. "Guatemala—Memory of Silence: Report of the Commission for Historical Clarification: Conclusions and Recommendations (February 1999)." *Die Friedens-Warte* 74, no. 4 (1999): 511–47. http://www.jstor.org/stable/23778631.

Conger, Robert D. "Porfirio Díaz and the Church Hierarchy, 1876–1911." PhD diss., University of New Mexico, 1985.

Escandón, María Amparo. *Esperanza's Box of Saints*. New York: Scribner Paperback Fiction, 1999.

Espinosa, Aurelio M. "New-Mexican Spanish Folk-Lore." *Journal of American Folklore* 23, no. 90 (1910): 395–418. https://doi.org/10.2307/534325.

Espinosa, J. Manuel. "The Origin of the Penitentes of New Mexico: Separating Fact from Fiction." *Catholic Historical Review* 79, no. 3 (1993): 454–77.

Esses, Victoria M., Stelian Medianu, and Andrea S. Lawson. "Uncertainty, Threat, and the Role of the Media in Promoting the Dehumanization of Immigrants and Refugees." *Journal of Social Issues* 69, no. 3 (September 2013): 518–36. https://doi.org/10.1111/josi.12027.

Fallon, Paul. "Staging a Protest: Fiction, Experience, and the Narrator's Shifting Position in *Las aventuras de Don Chipote o Cuando los pericos mamen*." *Confluencia* 23, no. 1 (2007): 115–27.

Galtung, Johan. "Violence, Peace, and Peace Research." *Journal of Peace Research* 6, no. 3 (1969): 167–91. https://doi.org/10.1177/002234336900600301.

Garcílazo, Jeffrey Marcos. *Traqueros: Mexican Railroad Workers in the United States, 1870 to 1930*. Denton: University of North Texas Press, 2012.

Gilliland, Frank D., William C. Hunt, Marla Pardilla, and Charles R. Key. "Uranium Mining and Lung Cancer among Navajo Men in

New Mexico and Arizona, 1969 to 1993." *Journal of Occupational and Environmental Medicine* 42, no. 3 (March 2000): 278–83. https://doi.org/10.1097/00043764-200003000-00008.

Goldsmith, Pat Rubio, Mary Romero, Raquel Rubio Goldsmith, Manual Escobedo, and Laura Khoury. "Ethno-Racial Profiling and State Violence in a Southwest Barrio." *AZTLÁN* 34, no. 1 (March 2009): 93–123.

Gómez, Myrriah M. "Toward a Chola Consciousness: Examining Nuclear Colonialism in *Lunar Braceros, 2125-2148*." *Science Fiction Studies* 48, no. 3 (November 2021): 500–16. https://doi.org/10.1353/sfs.2021.0071.

González, John M. "The Whiteness of the Blush: Cultural Politics of Racial Formation in *The Squatter and the Don*." In *María Amparo Ruiz de Burton: Critical and Pedagogical Perspectives*, edited by Amelia Maria de la Luz Montes and Anne Elizabeth Goldman, 153–68. Lincoln: University of Nebraska Press, 2004.

Guidotti-Hernández, Nicole Marie. *Unspeakable Violence: Remapping U.S. and Mexican National Imaginaries*. Latin America Otherwise: Languages, Empires, Nations. Durham, NC: Duke University Press, 2011.

Gutiérrez, Ramón A., and Elliott Young. "Transnationalizing Borderlands History." *Western Historical Quarterly* 41, no. 1 (2010): 26–53.

Herrera-Sobek, María. "Epidemics, Epistemophilia, and Racism: Ecological Literary Criticism and *The Rag Doll Plagues*." *Bilingual Review* 20, no. 3 (September 1995): 99–108. https://www.jstor.org/stable/25745304.

Hing, Bill Ong. "Mistreating Central American Refugees: Repeating History in Response to Humanitarian Challenges." *Hastings Race and Poverty Law Journal* 17 (2020): 359–98.

Holden, William Curry. *Teresita*. Owning Mills, MD, Stemmer House Publishers, 1978.

hooks, bell. *Yearning: Race, Gender, and Cultural Politics*. New York: Routledge, Taylor & Francis, 2015.

Hu-Dehart, Evelyn. "Development and Rural Rebellion: Pacification of the Yaquis in the Late 'Porfiriato.'" *Hispanic American Historical Review* 54, no. 1 (1974): 72–93.

Johnson, Adriana. "An Excess of Visibility, a Scarcity of Water." *Discourse* 43, no. 2 (Spring 2021): 189–215. https://doi.org/10.13110/discourse.43.2.0189.

Johnson, Benjamin H. "The Cosmic Race in Texas: Racial Fusion, White Supremacy, and Civil Rights Politics." *Journal of American History* 98, no. 2 (2011): 404–19.

Johnson, Leigh. "Covert Wars in the Bedroom and Nation: Motherwork, Transnationalism, and Domestic Violence in Black Widow's Wardrobe and Mother Tongue." *Meridians: Feminism, Race, Transnationalism* 11, no. 2 (2013): 149–71.

Kaplan, Caren, Norma Alarcón, and Minoo Moallem, eds. *Between Woman and Nation: Nationalisms, Transnational Feminisms, and the State.* Durham, NC: Duke University Press, 1999.

Kanellos, Nicolás. Introduction to Vanegas, *Adventures of Don Chipote*, xi–xxvii.

Keller, Gary. *Contemporary Chicana and Chicano Art: Artists, Works, Culture, and Education.* Tempe, AZ: Bilingual Press/Editorial Bilingue, 2002.

La Cueva Salcedo, Horacio de. "Environmental Violence and Its Consequences." *Latin American Perspectives* 42, no. 5 (September 2015): 19–26, https://doi.org/10.1177/0094582X15585116.

Lavender, Isiah, III. *Race in American Science Fiction.* Bloomington: Indiana University Press, 2011.

Lyon-Johnson, Kelli. "Acts of War, Acts of Memory: 'Dead-Body Politics' in US Latina Novels of the Salvadoran Civil War." *Latino Studies* 3, no. 2 (July 2005): 205–25.

Maringer, Johannes. "Priests and Priestesses in Prehistoric Europe." *History of Religions* 17, no. 2 (1977): 101–20. https://doi.org/10.1086/462783.

Martín, Desirée A. *Borderlands Saints: Secular Sanctity in Chicano/a and Mexican Culture.* Latinidad: Transnational Cultures in the United States. New Brunswick, NJ: Rutgers University Press, 2014.

Martínez, Demetria. *Confessions of a Berlitz-Tape Chicana.* Norman: University of Oklahoma Press, 2005.

———. *Mother Tongue.* New York: One World Books, 1994.

———. "Nativity: For Two Salvadoran Women, 1986–1987." *Bilingual Review/La Revista Bilingüe* 14, no. 1 (1987): 132.

Merla-Watson, Cathryn Josefina, and B. V. Olguín, eds. *Altermundos: Latin@ Speculative Literature, Film, and Popular Culture.* Los Angeles: UCLA Chicano Studies Research Center Press, 2017.

Miller, Larisa K. "The Secret Treaties with California's Indians." *Prologue* 45, no. 3-4 (2013): 38-45. https://www.archives.gov/files/publications/prologue/2013/fall-winter/treaties.pdf.

Mohanty, Chandra. *Feminism without Borders: Decolonizing Theory, Practicing Solidarity*. Durham, NC: Duke University Press, 2003.

Morales, Alejandro. *The Rag Doll Plagues*. Houston: Arte Público, 1994.

Musalo, Karen. "El Salvador: Root Causes and Just Asylum Policy Responses." *Hastings Race and Poverty Law Journal* 18, no. 2 (June 2021): 178-264.

Nava, Alex. "Teresa Urrea: Mexican Mystic, Healer, and Apocalyptic Revolutionary." *Journal of the American Academy of Religion* 73, no. 2 (2005): 497-519.

Nolan-Ferrel, Catherine. "Pedimos Posada: Local Mediators and Guatemalan Refugees in Mexico, 1978-1984." *Historia Crítica* 80 (2021): 153-78. https://doi.org/10.7440/histcrit80.2021.08.

Olguín, B. V. "Contrapuntal Cyborgs? The Ideological Limits and Revolutionary Potential of Latin@ Science Fiction." In Merla-Watson and Olguín, *Altermundos*, 128-44.

Orsi, Richard J. *Sunset Limited: The Southern Pacific Railroad and the Development of the American West*. Berkeley: University of California Press, 2005.

Paik, A. Naomi. "Abolitionist Futures and the US Sanctuary Movement." *Race & Class* 59, no. 2 (Fall 2017): 3-25. https://doi.org/10.1177/0306396817717858.

Payen-Variéras, Evelyne. "Gilded-Age Entrepreneurs and Local Notables: The Case of the California 'Big Four,' 1861-1877." *Transatlantica* no. 1 (2013): 1-19. https://doi.org/10.4000/transatlantica.6507.

Perez, Domino Renee. *There Was a Woman: La Llorona from Folklore to Popular Culture*. Austin: University of Texas Press, 2008.

Pérez, Emma. *The Decolonial Imaginary: Writing Chicanas into History*. Theories of Representation and Difference. Bloomington: Indiana University Press, 1999.

Pérez, Laura E. *Chicana Art: The Politics of Spiritual and Aesthetic Altarities*. Objects/Histories. Durham, NC: Duke University Press, 2007.

———. "*El desorden*, Nationalism, and Chicana/o Aesthetics." In Kaplan, Alarcón, and Moallem, *Between Woman and Nation*, 19-46.

Pulido, Laura. "Geographies of Race and Ethnicity III: Settler Colonialism and Nonnative People of Color." *Progress in Human Geography* 42, no. 2 (2018): 309–18.

Raab, Kelley A. *When Women Become Priests: The Catholic Women's Ordination Debate.* New York: Columbia University Press, 2000.

Rabuzzi, Kathryn Allen. *The Sacred and the Feminine: Toward a Theology of Housework.* New York: Seabury, 1982.

Ramírez, Catherine S. "Deus ex Machina: Tradition, Technology, and the Chicanafuturist Art of Marion C. Martinez." *Aztlán* 29, no. 2 (Fall 2004): 55–92. https://www.ingentaconnect.com/content/csrc/aztlan/2004/00000029/00000002/art00004.

Rivera, Lysa. "Future Histories and Cyborg Labor: Reading Borderlands Science Fiction after NAFTA." *Science Fiction Studies* 39, no. 3 (November 2012): 415–36. https://doi.org/10.5621/sciefictstud.39.3.0415.

Robinson, Amy. "From Private Healer to Public Threat: Teresa Urrea's Writings in The Hummingbird's Daughter and Queen of America." *Contracorriente: A Journal of Social History and Literature in Latin America* 13, no. 2 (2016): 240–63.

Robinson, William Wilcox. *Land in California: The Story of Mission Lands, Ranchos, Squatters, Mining Claims, Railroad Giants, Land Scrip, Homesteads.* Berkeley: University of California Press, 1979.

Rosaldo, Renato. *Culture and Truth: The Remaking of Social Analysis.* Boston: Beacon, 1989.

Ruiz de Burton, María Amparo. *The Squatter and the Don.* 1885. Houston: Arte Público, 1992.

Saldaña-Portillo, María Josefina. *Indian Given: Racial Geographies across Mexico and the United States.* Latin America Otherwise: Languages, Empire, Nations. Durham, NC: Duke University Press, 2016.

Saldívar, José David. *Border Matters: Remapping American Cultural Studies.* Berkeley: University of California Press, 1997.

Sandoval, Chela. *Methodology of the Oppressed.* Minneapolis: University of Minnesota Press, 2000.

Schoeffel, Melissa A. *Maternal Conditions: Reading Kingsolver, Castillo, Erdrich, and Ozeki.* American University Studies. Series XXIV, American Literature 78. New York: Peter Lang, 2008.

Segura, Denise A., and Beatriz M. Pesquera. "Beyond Indifference and Antipathy: The Chicana Movement and Chicana Feminist Discourse." *Aztlán* 19, no. 2 (September 1988): 69–92. https://www.ingentaconnect.com/content/csrc/aztlan/1988/00000019/00000002/art00004.

Seman, Jennifer Koshatka. *Borderlands Curanderos: The Worlds of Santa Teresa Urrea and Don Pedrito Jaramillo*. Austin: University of Texas Press, 2021.

Smythe, William E. *History of San Diego, 1542–1908*. San Diego: History Company, 1908. https://sandiegohistory.org/archives/books/smythe.

Steger, Manfred, and Ravi K. Roy. *Neoliberalism: A Very Short Introduction*. Oxford: Oxford University Press, 2010.

Stern, Alexandra Minna. *Eugenic Nation: Faults and Frontiers of Better Breeding in Modern America*. Berkeley: University of California Press, 2005.

Tisdale, Ashley B. "Transfigured Women: Race, Gender, and Disability in Alejandro Morales's *The Rag Doll Plagues*." *Chiricú Journal* 3, no. 2 (Spring 2019): 93–113. https://doi.org/10.2979/CHIRICU.3.2.07.

Trotter, Robert T., and Juan Antonio Chavira. *Curanderismo, Mexican American Folk Healing*. Athens: University of Georgia Press, 1981.

UN High Commissioner for Refugees. *Convention and Protocol Relating to the Status of Refugees*. Geneva: UNHCR Communications and Public Information Service, 2010. https://www.unhcr.org/sites/default/files/legacy-pdf/3b66c2aa10.pdf.

UN Office on Drugs and Crime. *Global Report on Trafficking in Persons 2022*. United Nations publication, Sales no.: E.23.IV.1, 2023.

Urrea, Luis Alberto. *The Hummingbird's Daughter: A Novel*. New York: Little, Brown, 2005.

US Environmental Protection Agency. *The Legacy of Abandoned Uranium Mines in the Grants Mineral Belt, New Mexico*. November 2011. https://www.epa.gov/sites/default/files/2015-08/documents/uranium-mine-brochure.pdf.

US General Accounting Office. *Treaty of Guadalupe Hidalgo: Findings and Possible Options Regarding Longstanding Community Land Grant Claims in New Mexico*. GAO-04-59. 2004.

Uzendoski, Andrew. "Narrating the Right to Health: Speculative Genre in Morales's *The Rag Doll Plagues*." In Merla-Watson and Olguín, *Altermundos*, 249–64.

Vanderwood, Paul J. *The Power of God against the Guns of Government: Religious Upheaval in Mexico at the Turn of the Nineteenth Century.* Stanford, CA: Stanford University Press, 1998.

———. "Santa Teresa: Mexico's Joan of Arc." In *The Human Tradition in Latin America: The 19th Century*, edited by Judith Ewell and William H. Beezley. Wilmington, DE: Scholarly Resources, 1989.

Van Metre, Thurman William. *Transportation in the United States.* Brooklyn, NY: Foundation Press, 1950.

Vasconcelos, José. *La raza cósmica: Mision de la raza iberoamericana, Argentina y Brasil.* 16th ed. Colección Austral: 802. Mexico City: Espasa-Calpe Mexicana, 1992.

Venegas, Daniel. *The Adventures of Don Chipote; or, When Parrots Breast-Feed.* 1928. Translated by Ethriam Cash Brammer and edited by Nicolás Kanellos. Houston: Arte Público, 2000.

Wiesel, Elie. "The Refugee." *CrossCurrents* 34, no. 4 (Winter 1984–1985): 385–90.

Zobl, Elke, and Elisabeth Klaus. "Cultural Production in Theory and Practice." *p|art|icipate* 10 (January 2012): 1–19. https://www.p-art-icipate.net.

INDEX

active shooter, 1–2
activists, characterizing, 74–79
affirmation, community through mirroring, 123–26
agabachadas (white identified), 92
Aguirre, Lauro, 21
Alarcón, Norma, 85, 87–88
Albuquerque Herald. See *Mother Tongue* (Martínez)
Almar, Don Mariano. See *Squatter and the Don, The* (Ruiz)
Amazon, 127
American Baptist Churches v. Thornburgh, 64
American Medical Association, 136, 166n24
American Southwest, 89–90
Anzaldúa, Gloria, 2, 81–82, 92, 112
Anzaldúa, Reynaldo (Rey), 119
Aquinas, Thomas, 91, 160n23
Arizona, 37
art, mirrors/mirroring in, 106–7; border violences, 107–9; at border wall, 113–18; Coatlicue state, 111–13; community affirmation, 123–26; critiques, 109–10; Moebius strip, 111–13
asylum seeker, 11; admission of, 63; defining, 58–62; term, 62–63
aventuras de Don Chipote, Las (Venegas), 11, 54–55; abuse of Mexican immigrants in, 48–54; dog owner situation in, 52–53; exploitation of Mexican immigrant workers, 53–54; migrant exploitation in, 49; narrative historicization in, 50–51; narrator interjections, 51–52; Papa Supply, 52; as protest novel, 48; railroad company representation in, 36–37; socio-history behind, 48–49; speaking directly to readers, 49; undressing in, 50
Avila, Modesta, 35

Barbour, G. W., 38
Barthes, Roland, 101
Behr P500-2 Seashore Dreams, 114
Berger, Kayley, 47
Big Four, 41–43, 46
biological determinism, 91
Black people, 7, 63
Black Widow's Wardrobe (Corpi), 86
Blanca. See *Esperanza's Box of Saints* (Escandón)
Blue Buster. See *Rag Doll Plagues, The* (Morales)
Border Brujo (Gómez-Peña), 109
border town, characterizing, 73
border wall, US-Mexico, 106–7; Coatlicue state and, 111–13; community affirmation, 123–26;

177

border wall (*continued*)
   critiquing, 109–10; mirrors and mirroring in, 113–18; Moebius strip and, 111–13; violences of, 107–9

Borderlands / La Frontera: The New Mestiza (Anzaldúa), 112

Borderlands Campaign, Sierra Club, 116

borderlands consciousness, 4, 9, 16, 18, 32–34, 51, 67–68, 81–82, 94, 118, 123–24, 128, 130–31, 143, 145, 149–52

borderlands history, transnationalizing, 18

Borderwall as Architecture: A Manifesto for the US-Mexico Boundary (Juárez), 124

Borrando la Frontera (Fernández), 12, 107, 114–18

Boyd, Consuelo, 31–32

Bracken, Rachel Conrad, 48–50

Burton, María Amparo Ruiz de, 11, 41, 49

Bush, George W., 109

California, 37–38, 40

California Land Act (1851), 37–38

Carter administration, 62

Castillo, Ana, 11, 81–82, 92–93

Catholic Church, 15, 22–26, 89–91, 104

Cavazos, José Alfredo, 119

CBP. *See* Customs and Border Protection

Center for Biological Diversity, 116–17

Center for Disease Control and Prevention (CDC), 122

Central Americans, 125; protecting collective memory of, 66–74; refugees, 62–66; sanctuary movement and, 74–79

Central Pacific Railroad Company, 40

Centro de Investigación Científica y de Educación Superior de Ensenada, 108

Cervantes, Miguel de, 96

Chabram-Dernersesian, Angie, 3

Chapablanco, Pablo, 70–72

Chávez, Cruz, 23, 33

Chicana Art: The Politics of Spiritual and Aesthetic Altarities (Pérez), 103

"Chicana Feminism: In the Tracks of 'The' Native Woman" (Alarcón), 87–88

Chicanafuturism, 12, 148; COVID-19 pandemic and, 127–28; cyborg trope and, 139–47; ecological devastation and, 132–39; making waves in tranquil waters, 130–32; neoliberalism and, 128–30

Chicanx, 80–81, 106, 113, 126, 151; critiquing border, 109–10; La Madre and, 89–92

Chinese Exclusion Act, 48

Christ, Jesus, 90–91, 102

Christchurch Mosque, 1

Christianity, term, 159n19

Chung, Gabi. *See Rag Doll Plagues, The* (Morales)

citizen-subject, 5

Ciudad Juárez, 1, 8, 124, 137, 146, 149–50

C. Loyal. *See* Burton, María Amparo Ruiz de Coatlicue, 112

Coatlicue state, 111–13, 123–24
cognitive estrangement, 131
collective memory, protecting: media scrutinization, 73–74; memory community, 66–67; salvaging stories, 67–68; USBP authority, 69–72; writing about racialization, 68–69
Colorado, 37
Colton, David D., 46
Commission for Historical Clarification, 65
communities: affirming through mirroring, 123–26; Brown and Black, 72, 121; depicting as violent, 2–5; Latinx, 2, 74; local, 35, 114, 120; marginalized, 7, 9, 11, 128–30, 150; racializing, 8
Confessions of a Berlitz-Tape Chicana (Martínez), 11, 58, 66; introduction to, 67–68; racialization-criminalization process, 69–70; and sanctuary movement, 76–79
Conger, Robert D., 25
Congress, US, 115–16
Contemporary Chicana and Chicano Art: Artists, Works, Culture, and Education (Keller), 110
Convention and Protocol Related to the Status of Refugees, 61
Cornell Law Review, 70–71
Corpi, Lucha, 86
Cortés, Hernán, 160n28
COVID-19, 108, 113, 120–22, 123, 127–28, 136, 140–42
criminalization, refugees, 79; 1980s

Central American refugees, 62–66; example of, 56–58; language of, 58–62; protecting collective memory, 66–74; racialization-criminalization process, 69–70; sanctuary movement, 74–79
critiques, border, 109–10
Crocker, Charles, 41
cruelty, responding to nonviolence with, 35–36
Cubillas, Alberto, 28
cultural production, 8–13, 28, 36, 70, 104, 128, 131, 148, 151
curandera, 10. *See also* Urrea, Teresa (Teresita)
Customs and Border Protection (CBP), 6, 56–58, 141
cyberbraceros (cyborg laborers), 142–43
cyborg, trope, 139; in *Lunar Braceros, 2125-2148*, 140–42; in *Rag Doll Plagues*, 145–49; in *Sleep Dealer*, 142–45
Cybracero. See *Sleep Dealer* (film)

Daily Herald, 21
Daily, The, 144–45
Davis, Jefferson, 39
Declaration of Independence, 63
Declaration on the Question of Admission of Women to the Ministerial Priesthood, 160n21
dehumanization, cyborg trope and, 139–47
Delgado, Teresa, 151

Department of Homeland Security (DHS), 104, 119–20
Department of Justice (DOJ), 62
DHS. *See* Department of Homeland Security
Día de los Niños (Children's Day), 123
Díaz, Porfirio, 14, 16, 18–19, 21; and Yaqui pacification program, 26–30
disruptive cultural mappings, 4
division, violence of, 107–8, 119–22
DOJ. *See* Department of Justice
Domecq, Brianda, 15
drifty, 101

ecological devastation: in *Lunar Braceros, 2125-2148*, 138–39; in *Rag Doll Plagues*, 133–36; in *Sleep Dealer*, 136–38
8chan, 1
El Paso Bath Riots, 50
El Paso, Texas, active shooter in, 1–2
El Salvador, 57; refugees from, 64–66
Emrick, Gail, 120
Environmental Protection Agency (EPA), 138–39
environmental violence, 108
EOIR. *See* Executive Office for Immigration Review
EPA. *See* Environmental Protection Agency
Erasing the Border (Fernández). *See Borrando la Frontera* (Fernández)
ERRE, Marcos Ramírez, 12, 107, 123, 126
Escandón, María Amparo, 11, 81–82, 92–93
Esparanza. *See Esperanza's Box of Saints* (Escandón)

Esperanza's Box of Saints (Escandón), 11–12, 81–82; carving out sacred spaces, 97–104; defying La Madre, 89–97; spiritual authority of La Madre, 82–85; transnational violence in, 87–89; transnational Chicana feminism in, 85–86
Espinosa, Aurelio M., 161n31
Esses, Victoria M., 73–74
Executive Office for Immigration Review (EOIR), 64
exile, Teresa Urrea, 30–32

familia crossing, image, 110
Farabundo Martí National Liberation Front (FMLN), 65
Father Gastélum, 22–26
Father Jerome. *See So Far from God* (Castillo)
Felicia, Doña. *See So Far from God* (Castillo)
feminism, Chicana, 85–86
Fernández, Ana Teresa, 12, 107, 114–16, 126
fibroblast migration, 149–52
Fife, John, 75
FMLN. *See* Farabundo Martí National Liberation Front
Foucault, Michel, 5
Fragoso, character, 139–40
Friendship Park, 123–24
fronterizos, 107

Galtung, Johan, 6, 15, 61–62, 80, 107, 130
Garcia, Margarita Certeza, 12, 107, 123, 126

Garcílazo, Jeffrey Marcos, 48
gender roles, 80–82
gente fronteriza, la, 13
Gilbert, Samuel, 121
global structure, 5
Golden Age of Controlled Capitalism, 129
Gómez-Peña, Guillermo, 109, 116, 123
Gómez, Myrriah M., 138
González, John M., 46–47
Gordon, Alan, 69–70
Gould-Huntington Agreement, 42–43
Gould, Jay, 42
Greaser Act (1855), 47
Great Depression, 129
Guardian, 121
Guatemala, 57; discrimination faced by, 68–69; violent conflict in, 64–66
Guidotti-Hernández, Nicole, 7–8, 29
Gutiérrez, Ramón A., 18

hacendado, 16, 27–28, 41, 46, 156n16
Herrera-Sobek, María, 132, 133
Herweck, Stefanie, 109
Hicks, Emily, 109
Hispanic appearance, legal classification, 70–71
Holden, William Curry, 14–15, 22–23
hooks, bell, 98
Hopkins, Mark, 41
Hu-DeHart, Evelyn, 26–29
human trafficking, UN report on, 88–89
Hummingbird's Daughter, The (Urrea), 10–11, 33–34; Father Gastélum in, 22–26; fictionalized media exposure, 20–22; overview of, 14–16; sections of, 20; Urrea as historical religious icon, 16–20; Urrea exile, 30–32; Urrea-Gastélum exchange, 23–24; violence perpetuated in, 19–20; Yaqui pacification program and, 26–30
Huntington, Collis Potter, 41–46

ICE. *See* Immigration and Customs Enforcement
imagined community of a nation, 3–5, 7, 10, 36, 81
immigrants, abuse of, 48–54
Immigration and Customs Enforcement (ICE), 6
Immigration and Nationality Act (INA), 59
Immigration and Naturalization Service (INS), 64
INA. *See* Immigration and Nationality Act
Independiente, El, 21
Indian savage, language, 63
indígena, 19
indio bárbaro, stereotype, 27–28
Ingenioso Hidalgo Don Quijote de la Mancha, El (Cervantes), 96–97
insólita historia de la Santa de Cabora, La (Domecq), 15
Inter-American Human Rights Commission, 65
Inter-American Symposium on Sanctuary, 58

invisibilization, violence, 148; Chicanafuturism, 130–32; cyborg trope and, 139–47; ecological devastation and, 132–39; neoliberalism and, 128–30; overview, 127–28
Izábal, Rafael, 29

Jaramillo, Don Pedrito. See *Rag Doll Plagues, The* (Morales)
Johnson, Richard, 9
Juárez, Ciudad, 8, 124, 149–50

Kanellos, Nicolás, 48–49
Kansas, 37
Kaplan, Caren, 85
Keller, Gary, 110
Klaus, Elisabeth, 9
Klein, James, 144–45

La Boquilla Dam, 137–38
labor, invisibilization of, 139, 148; in *Lunar Braceros, 2125-2148*, 140–42; in *Rag Doll Plagues*, 145–49; in *Sleep Dealer*, 142–45
Lacan, Jacques, 111
land: acquisition of, 37–38; reclassifying as public, 40–41; right-of-way, 40; rights, 37–41; surveying of, 39
language, criminalization, 58–62
latent violence, 61–62, 79
Lavín, Guillermo, 140
Lawson, Andrea S., 73–74
liberation theology, 154n9
limpia, 102–3

Llorente, Juan Antonio. See *Rag Doll Plagues, The* (Morales)
Llorona, La, figure, 92–93, 160n28
Loca, La. See *So Far from God* (Castillo)
Los Angeles Times, 35, 120
Los Ganados y Lana Cooperative, 100
Lunar Braceros, 2125-2148 (Pita), 12, 128, 148; cyborgs in, 140–42; ecological devastation in, 138–39
Lyon-Johnson, Kelli, 66–67

Madre, La: defiance of, 89–97; overview of, 80–82; rising spiritual experience, 104–5; sacred places, 97–104; spiritual authority of, 82–85; transnational violence, 87–89; transnational Chicana feminism, 85–86
Malinche, figure, 92–93
malogra, la, 161n31. See also *So Far from God* (Castillo)
Manuel, Andrés, 138
Marcela. See *Ingenioso Hidalgo Don Quijote de la Mancha, El* (Cervantes)
marginalization, defying, 3–4, 6, 8, 92
Maria. See *Mother Tongue* (Martínez)
Maringer, Johannes, 98–99
Martín, Desireé A., 16
Martínez, Demetria, 11, 58, 66–74; and sanctuary movement, 74–76
Mayos, 15, 19–20, 26–27, 30–31, 33–34
McKee, Redick, 38
media exposure, fictionalizing, 20–22

media scrutinization, 73–74
Medianu, Stelian, 73–74
Memo. See *Sleep Dealer* (film)
memory community, 66–67. See also collective memory, protecting
mestizaje, 19
Metre, T. W. Van, 39
Mexicali, 127, 141
Mexican-American War, 37
Mexican Brown, legal classification, 72
Mexican cultural patterns, maintenance of, 91
Mexican Revolution, 19, 48
Mictlan, 110
Mictlantecuhtli, 110
migrant worker communities, 127
mirroring: affirming community through, 123–25; border wall art, 113–18
mirrors, border wall art, 106–7, 113–18
Moallem, Minoo, 85
Moebius strip, 111–13, 123, 125, 126
Mohanty, Chandra, 85–86
Molina, Olegario, 28
Mona, La. See *Rag Doll Plagues, The* (Morales)
Morales, Alejandro, 12, 28, 132, 133
Mother Tongue (Martínez), 11, 58, 66; global citizens in, 86; media scrutinization, 73–74; USBP authority in, 72–73; writing about racialization in, 68; writing about racialization through, 68–69
mother-pastora, 96–97, 102–3
mother, figure. See Madre, La
Musalo, Karen, 63

NAFTA. See North American Free Trade Agreement
narrative, historicizing, 50–51, 53
narrator, interjection of, 51–52. See also *aventuras de Don Chipote, Las* (Venegas)
National Museum of Anthropology, 112
National Origins Act (1924), 48
nation-states, 3, 10, 32, 58, 86, 111–12, 114, 124
"Nativity" (poem), 76–79
Navajo Nation, 139
negligence, violence of, 108–9, 119–22
neoliberalism, 128–30
Nevada, 37
New Mexico, 37
New York Times, 121, 144
New Zealand, 1
Nicol, Scott, 116
Nogales, Arizona, 120
Nolan-Ferell, Catherine, 69
nonviolence, responding with cruelty to, 35–36
Norris, Ned, Jr., 118
North American Free Trade Agreement (NAFTA), 129–30, 137
nuclear colonialism, 138–39
nuclear family, concept, 86

Obama, Barack, 109
Obrador, López, 138
Office of Refugee Resettlement (ORR), 60
Oklahoma, 37
Olguín, B. V., 131

"On the Other Side of the Mexican Mirror" (Gómez-Peña), 112–13
Organ Pipe Cactus National Monument, 118
ORR. *See* Office of Refugee Resettlement

Pacific Railway Act, 39
pacification programs, Yaquis and, 26–30
Paik, A. Naomi, 76
Papa Supply, 52. See also *aventuras de Don Chipote, Las* (Venegas)
Payen-Variéras, Evelyne, 421
Penitentes, 159n13
Pepenador, El. See *Rag Doll Plagues, The* (Morales)
Pérez, Emma, 18
Pérez, Laura E., 80, 103
personal violence, 7, 130
Pesquera, Beatriz, 91
Phillips, Dave, 144
Pita, Beatrice, 12, 128, 132
Porfiriato, 24–25
Power of God against the Guns of Government, The (Vanderwood), 14
"Priests and Priestesses in Prehistoric Europe" (Maringer), 98–99
privileged enslavement, 147
protest novel. See *aventuras de Don Chipote, Las* (Venegas)
Public Land Commission, 38
Puerto Rican Decolonial Theology: A Prophesy Freedom (Delgado), 151
Pulido, Laura, 29, 32

"'Queremos Vivir': The Workers Who Wouldn't Die for the Pentagon," report, 141–42
querencia, 13
"Question of Admission of Women to the Ministerial Priesthood," 90–91

Raab, Kelley A., 90–91
Rabuzzi, Kathryn A., 99
Rael, Ronald, 12, 107, 124
Rag Doll Plagues, The (Morales), 12–13, 128, 148; cyborgs in, 145–49; ecological devastation in, 133–36
railroads corporations, complicity of: industry cruelty, 41–47; land rights, 37–41; Mexican immigrant abuse, 48–54; overview, 35–37; public domain, 37–41; US expansion, 37–41
Ramírez, Catherine S., 131
Ramirez, Rudy. See *Sleep Dealer* (film)
raza cósmica, la, 19
"Reaching the Shore" (Lavín), 140
Reagan administration, 62, 65
Re/flecting the Border (Garcia), 12, 107, 123–24
Reflections (Fife), 75
refugee, 11
Refugee Act (1980), 60, 62–64, 66
refugees: admission of, 63;

criminalizing, 62–66; defining, 58–62; example of, 56–58; sanctuary movement and, 74–79. *See also* criminalization, refugees
Remer-Thamert, Glen, 76
Report to Congress on Proposed Refugee Admissions for Fiscal Year 2021, 60
Revolutionary Government Junta, 65
Revueltas, Gregorio. See *Rag Doll Plagues, The* (Morales)
Richardson Construction Company, 28
Rio Grande Valley, 109
Río Yaqui Valley, 22, 28–29
Rivera, Alex, 12, 128, 132
Rivera, Lysa, 132, 139–40
River Bend Resort and Golf Club, 119
Robinson, Amy, 21
Robinson, William Wilcox, 40
Rodriguez, Roberto, 69
Roe v. Wade, 151
Roman Catholic Church, 159n19
romerías, 14
Romero, Carlos Humberto, 65
Rosa M., 110
Roy, Ravi K., 129–30
Ruiz, María Amparo, 36

Sacred and the Feminine: Toward a Theology of Housework, The (Rabuzzi), 99
Sacred Jump, The (Underwood), 109–10
sacred spaces, La Madre, 97–104
sacrilegious violence, 108
Sagrada Familia de Aztlan, La (Rosa M.), 110
saguaro plant, 117–18
Saint Judas Thaddeus. See *So Far from God* (Castillo)
Salas, Esequiel, 120
Salcedo, Horacio de la Cueva, 108
Saldaña-Portillo, Josefina, 27
Saldívar, José David, 3–4, 8–9
Sánchez, Rosaura, 12, 128, 132
sanctuary movement, criminalizing, 74–79
Sandoval, Chela, 101
San Francisco Chronicle, 127–28
San Quentin State Prison, 35
Santa Ana Del Rio. See *Sleep Dealer* (film)
Santa Ana National Wildlife Refuge, 109, 115–17
Santa Ana Wildlife Reserve, 118
Santa de Cabora, La. See Urrea, Teresa
Santa Fe Magazine, 53
Santa Fe Railroad Company, 53
"Santa Teresa: Mexico's Joan of Arc" (Vanderwood), 17–18
SARS-CoV-2 virus, 108
Scarlet Room, 103
Schoeffel, Melissa, 93
Sculpture Nature, 114
Secure Fence Act (2006), 124
seesaw, representation, 124–25
Segura, Denise, 91
Seman, Jennifer Koshatka, 17, 135

Sierra Club, 109
Sleep Dealer (film), 12, 128, 148; cyborgs in, 142–45; ecological devastation in, 136–38
So Far from God (Castillo), 11, 81–82; carving out sacred spaces, 97–104; defying La Madre, 89–97; spiritual authority of La Madre, 82–85; transnational Chicana feminism in, 85–86; transnational violence in, 87–89
Sofia. See *So Far from God* (Castillo)
Soledad. See *Mother Tongue* (Martínez)
somatic violence, 6
Sonoran Desert, 117–18
Sonora Railway, 31–32
Southern Pacific Railroad, 40
Southside Presbyterian Church, 75
sovereign structure, 5
Spanish Empire, 28, 134
spell, breaking. See collective memory, protecting
spiritual authority: defiance of, 89–97; manifestations of, 82–85; sacred places and, 97–103; transnational Chicana feminism and, 85–86; transnational violence, 87–89
Squatter and the Don, The (Burton), 11; appealing to Stanford, 43–45; conclusion of, 45–46; exposing violence, 46–47; industry cruelty portrayed in, 41–47; investing in Texas Pacific Railroad, 43–45; plot of, 41–42; railroad company representation in, 36–37

Stanford, Leland, 41, 43–45
Starbucks, 127
Steger, Manfred, 129–30
Stern, Alexandra Minna, 50–51
structural violence, 1, 6–8, 130; railroad construction and, 35–55
Summa Theologica (Aquinas), 91
Suvin, Darko, 131

Tariff Act (1930), 141
Tedford, Matthew Harrison, 114
Teeter-Totter Wall (Rael), 12, 107, 124
Teresita (Holden), 15, 22–23
Texas, 37
Texas Pacific Railroad, investing in, 41–47. See also *Squatter and the Don, The* (Burton)
TGH. See Treaty of Guadalupe Hidalgo
Tigers of Tomóchic, 23
Tijuana, 84, 97, 104, 109, 114, 123, 137, 141–43
Tisdale, Ashley B., 145–46
Title 42, public health order, 121–22
Tohono O'odham, tribe, 117–18
Tomé, New Mexico. See *So Far from God* (Castillo)
Tomochic Rebellion, 14
Tomochic Uprising, 23
Torres, Aureliano, 27
trafficking, defining, 159n15
tranquil waters, 148; cyborg trope and, 139–47; making waves in, 130–32; of neoliberalism, 128–30
transcontinental railroad, 39–41
transnational Chicana feminism, 85–86

transnational violence, 87–89

traqueros, 48. See also *aventuras de Don Chipote, Las* (Venegas)

Treaty of Guadalupe Hidalgo (TGH), 27, 77, 119

Trump administration, 59, 103, 115, 117–18, 119, 120, 128

Trump presidency, 113

Trump, Donald J., 1, 106, 119–20, 122

Underwood, Consuelo Jiménez, 109–10

Union Pacific Railroad Company, 39–40

United Nations, 65, 88, 118

United States, 26, 57; Chicanx identity and, 80; complicity with railroad corporations, 35–55; conceptualization of ideal citizen, 36; Guatemalan government and, 65–66; involvement in violent conflicts, 64–66; land expansion, 37–41; origin mythology, 10; Salvadoran refugees and, 64–66

United States v. Brignoni-Ponce, 69–70

United States v. Martinez-Fuerte, 71

Universal Declaration of Human Rights (1948), 61

Unspeakable Violence: Remapping U.S. and Mexican National Imaginaries (Guidotti), 7

Urrea, Luis Alberto, 10–11, 20–22, 30, 31, 33

Urrea, Teresa, 14–16, 33–34; activism of, 17–18; Catholic Church and, 22–26; early life of, 16–17; exiling of, 30–32; Father Gastélum juxtaposition, 22–26; fictionalized version of, 20–22; healing powers of, 17; as historical religious icon, 16–20; as political exile, 18; story of, 20–22; time period of, 18–19; Yaqui pacification program and, 26–30

Urrea, Tomás, 14, 16–17, 22, 31

US Border Patrol (USBP), 69–72

US Department of Agriculture, 117–18

US Immigration Service, 50

US–Mexico borderlands: border wall art, 106–26; Coatlicue state, 106–26; cultural production of, 8–13; fibroblast migration, 149–52; imagined community of, 3; as inverted cartography, 113; invisibilization of violence, 127–48; Moebius strip, 106–26; perpetuating violence in, 4–5; quotients of power in, 5–6; refugee criminalization, 56–79; Teresa Urrea representation, 14–34; transitional female spiritual leadership, 80–105; types of violence in, 6–8; United States-railroad complicity, 35–55; violence in, 2–5; violence of division and neglect along, 119–22

US Public Health Service (USPHS), 50

Utah, 37

Uzendoski, Andrew, 131

INDEX / 187

Vanderwood, Paul J., 14, 16–21, 24
Vasconcelos, José, 19
vendidas (sell-outs), 92
Venegas, Daniel, 11, 36
violence: environmental, 108; invisibilization of, 127–48; marginalization constituting, 6; of border, 107–9; of division, 107–8, 119–22; of neglect, 121–22; of negligence, 108–9, 119–22; personal, 130; power structure perpetuating, 3–4; sacrilegious, 108; structural, 130; transnational, 87–89; types of, 6–7; in US-Mexico borderlands, 2–5

Washington Post, 103
water, privatization of, 136–38. See also *Sleep Dealer* (film)

When Women Become Priests (Raab), 90
"Whiteness of the Blush, The," 46–47
Wild West, 100
Women of All Red Nations, 138
Wozencraft, O. M., 38
Wyoming, 37

Yaquis, 15, 18–20, 31, 33–34; pacification program of, 26–30
Yearning: Race, Gender, and Cultural Politics (hooks), 98
Young, Elliott, 18

Zobl, Elke, 9
Zyklon B, 121

www.ingramcontent.com/pod-product-compliance
Lightning Source LLC
Chambersburg PA
CBHW030103170825
30846CB00001B/12